,50

FOODS *of the* ORIENT

India

Introduced by Sharmini Tiruchelvam

Marshall Cavendish London & New York

Picture Credits

Patrick Cochrane	58
Alan Duns	10/1, 63, 99, 103/4, 107
Mark Edwards	B.C.8
Gascoigne/Robert Harding Associates	8
Tom Hanley	6
Jerry Harpur	43
Denis Hughes-Gilbey	72/3
Paul Kemp	16/7, 37, 69, 81
Don Last	28
Roger Phillips	13, 31, 35, 41, 44/5, 47, 53, 56/7, 60, 65, 74, 77, 78, 82/3, 90, 94, 96, 100
Iain Reid	22/3, 24/5, 50/1, 87
Red Saunders	32

Edited by Isabel Moore
and Jonnie Godfrey

Published by Marshall Cavendish Books Limited
58 Old Compton Street
London W1V 5PA

© Marshall Cavendish Limited 1978

This volume first published 1978

Printed in Great Britain

ISBN 0 85685 483 2

CONTENTS

INTRODUCTION TO INDIA

Sharmini Tiruchelvam

Asked what single factor above others had formed the world of man as we know it, my father, a distinguished surgeon, answered unhesitatingly: 'Spices and the search for the Spice-lands'. An apparently flippant answer.

Yet not so on examination. For it was in attempting to discover the route to the fabled spice-rich Indies that the Old World mounted the greatest land search ever and discovered the two Americas, the West Indies and the two pre-canal routes round the Cape of Good Hope and Cape Horn. These discoveries of vast new land masses with their attendant wealth altered horizons in every sense; it changed the path of civilization. It also led Britain and Europe to the East and to the massive colonizing of the latter by the former. But, in the end and at least on the culinary level, it was the East which conquered the palate of the West, for 'curry' in some form or other has become a virtually universal dish.

It is one of the basic Western misconceptions about Indian cuisine that curry is the sum total of it – everything else being merely an extension or variation on the theme. Another is a curious belief that there is some magical, single, all-purpose mixture called a curry powder. A third, that spices are basically harmful, bad for the stomach, the liver, the kidneys, the complexion. (Nothing could be farther from the truth for, in fact, the original functions of spices in cooking were primarily as preservatives and medicinal cures.) In India, as elsewhere, their use gradually evolved from curative to aromatic so that it is now probably true to say that it is the proportionate assembling, method of preparation, combining techniques and blending with one another, and with other ingredients within each recipe, that is literally the very essence of the classic cooking of India and its neighbour Sri Lanka. This mixture of spices is called *masala*.

There is a great mystique about *masala* in the West although its combination is simplicity itself. At their most basic *masalas* are a combination of three types of aromatics – spices, herbs and seasonings. There are, of course, classic combinations but anyone can make up a *masala* with any combination – beginning with the simplest: a basic one-member-from-each-group arrangement (for example: fresh red chillis or paprika ground with crushed garlic, salt and lemon juice). You can then go on to more complex arrangements – and almost invariably discover that you have merely recreated an existing combination! But once certain traditional *masalas* have been mastered, there is nothing to stop you inventing your own dishes.

There is just one injunction: whether a dish be cooked or assembled raw, the *masala* must never taste 'raw'. This is simply a matter of knowing how much marinating or cooking time to allow for the spices especially, and experience will eventually teach when, with which and for how long; for different spices sometimes need attention separately depending on what they are being combined with. Often a quick, dry-pan roasting or 'tempering', in advance of use will suffice.

Some of India's finest cuisine has been developed, preserved and passed on from generation to generation, in fact within families. The recipes were taught practically; rarely, if ever, were they written down. There were of course the master-chefs who served in the palaces and with the great families. They were apprenticed for years to master-chefs before they qualified, so that once again the knowledge was handed down practically. Although considered great artists, even among them, there were almost none who could aspire to, far less claim, all-round proficiency, so great was the range. One man would specialize in *tandoor* cooking; another in the techniques of barbecuing and the preparation of the marinades; another would be a *korma* (considered the greatest art) expert, while yet another would excel in the cooking of *turrcurries* (curry cooking). Finally there was a whole magical world of the confectioner with his 'Arabian Nights' array of sweetmeats.

'The Hand Knows', they say, referring to that infallibility which usually develops with practice – if indeed it has not been there from the beginning – when almost without conscious thought an expert or experienced cook will stop adding a spice or condiment and proceed to the next stage of the work. Knowing the basic classic recipe is essential, but it is important, they say in the East, to know how the finished dish at its best should (a) smell (b) look like (c) taste and (d) have what texture – for instance, the meat of a *pasandah* should virtually melt in the mouth whereas the meat of a *tandoor* cooked chicken should be moist and tender but firm – in that order.

5

Regional Cooking

Setting aside personal variations, the subcontinent has as many different types of cooking as there are regions and provinces: Bengali, Punjabi (considered by many the best), Kashmiri, Sindhi, Asamese, Tamil, Hyderbadi, Goan to name only some. Each has its own favourite foods and idiosyncratic mixture of spices and other ingredients. The reasons for some are obvious: climate and terrain and the produce of that terrain according to the seasons; proximity to the seas, rivers and oceans and to the availability of foodstuffs from them. The people of Kerala for example, with a considerable sea coast, fisherfolk, have great sea-food cooks. The 'kool' of the South Indian (and Sri Lankan) Tamils is a rich bouillabaisse of sea foods, with powdered kernal of Palmyra palm – which grows in those lands – for thickening, together with sliced, barely cooked, crunchy young green beans – probably plucked straight off their runners that morning by the cook. Travellers, traders and invaders influenced the cuisine, too, and undoubtedly the greatest single influence on the formation of an haute cuisine in India, was the Moghuls.

The Moghuls came from the north, and it is interesting that one can clearly trace, in the magnificence of Moghlai cooking, the cooking of their wild nomad ancestors, the earlier twelfth century Mongols (who incidentally also influenced Northern Chinese cuisine) with their preference for mutton, skewered marinated meats which were the forerunners of tandoor foods, hot pots and pot roasts, together with all-purpose soured milk, the ancestor of yogurt.

The Moghul also brought with him his food taboos. A Muslim, he forbade the eating of pork, also no sea scavengers, no crustacea: similar taboos to those of the Jews, from the same part of the world. One realizes that there were reasons more commonsensical than the mindless proscription of bigots to which these taboos were often attributed. The religious teachers and leaders were also their society's elders, the general law and health-law givers. Certain animals carried diseases which affected man when he ate their flesh. They banned his eating of them. Pork was the chief of these.

It is interesting to note that nowhere in the Vedic Law does it ban the eating of beef. But the elders of India saw the possible decimation of cattle from their land and feared that the pullers of their ploughs and carts, the givers of their precious milk, would be made extinct. So those ancient ecologists declared the cow sacred and banned the eating of its flesh! Buddhism came with its injunctions to take no life whatsoever. With it

A busy, colourful scene in Calcutta where local delicacies can readily be obtained from street traders.

came into existence a great school of purely vegetarian cooking.

The Classic Methods and Styles

There are about fourteen main methods or techniques of cooking Indian dishes. Some of these, of course, have several subdivisions – for instance, there are four types of bhuna. Some also overlap one another as in the case of dummed-bhuna or korma-dohpeeazah, where each is a mixture of two or more techniques. To put it as simply as possible, they are: Currying – stewing; Dumming – steaming; Korma – braising (classically within a sealed pot); Bhuna – sautéeing and pot roasting; Talawa – deep-frying; Tandoori – tandoor oven cooking; Keebab – charcoal grilling (broiling); Oven baking and roasting of specially marinated foods and meat-stuffed breads; Tarka – a form of high-heat searing with ghee and glazing to finish; Parcha – rolled and stuffed meats; Dohpeeazah – the technique of adding onions, classically twice, (hence 'doh') but it can be three or more times throughout the cooking of a dish; Wrapped – 'en paupiette' – wrapped in smoked leaves such as banana leaves, or cooked encrusted in pastry as samosas; Bhogar – combining and assimilating the flavours belonging to two or more ingredients of a dish within a sealed pot; Koftas – minced (ground) meatballs.

Rice and Rice Cooking

There is no doubt that the most exquisitely assembled set of meat, vegetable and fish dishes can be ruined if the basis of the meal, the rice, is less than superb. As with everything else in life the quality of the starter materials matter. There are over a thousand varieties and sub-varieties of rice. The best for savoury rice cooking is Patna – a long-grain non-glutinous rice which cooks out each grain separately. The best again within this grouping are Basmati, Dehra Dun and Almora. There are all sorts of confusions about the various basic rice dishes. To summarize very simply: Plain boiled rice; Plain steamed rice; Mkhani or buttered rice. (The boiled or steamed rice, cooked, has ghee or butter and some delicate aromatics added to it. It is then put under foil or in a sealed dish and 'dummed' for a few minutes in the oven to allow the butter and aromatics to be absorbed.) A fourth type is pulaus, which range from plain to shahi degh pulau.

The basis of all pulaus is that the uncooked rice is first gently sautéed in ghee or butter until the grains become translucent. It is then always cooked in some sort of stock.

Classic biryanis are always flavoured and coloured with saffron. Turmeric is sometimes used as a substitute in cheaper versions. They always have the following combination of spices: cumin, coriander, cardamom seeds, whole black peppercorns, cinnamon and cloves. Twice as much butter

7

as for any of the other *pulaus* is used and twice as much meat or fish as the rice used for the dish.

Breads

Nan, the *tandoor* baked bread is the classic accompaniment for *tandoor* cooked meats. It is leavened bread made from white flour. The basic unleavened bread of the subcontinent – somewhat resembling the Mexican tortilla or a rough, very dry, thickish pancake and very tasty despite that description of it – is the *chapatti*. The thickest and coarsest form of it is called *roti*. The thin form of it is the classic *chapatti*. The thinnest and lightest form of it is the *phulka*. *Puris* are small round, sometimes merely bite-sized *phulkas* deep-fried until they are puffed out and airy light if done well. *Parathas* are heavier, layered, shallow-fried and may be either plain or stuffed with meats or vegetables, or both. All of the above are classically made with wholewheat flour (*atar*) or pounded barley, millet or buckwheat. They can also be made with rice flour, but this is less tasty and nutritious.

The South of India also boasts a fantastic array of breakfast 'breads' or hoppers, from the plain hopper to the milk hopper and the egg hopper. These are made with toddy leavening. String hoppers – like steamed platelets made of Chinese rice sticks – are made out of rice flour, as is *puttu*, a steamed unsweetened crumble pastry bread with coconut; *iddlis* – feather light, greyish, glancingly sour, soft crumpets are made of rice flour and lentils and *thosais* are like Scots oat-cakes. The list is endless.

Cooking ingredients

The Indians of the North, West and Central parts of India and the purist Jaffna Tamils of Sri Lanka all cook exclusively in ghee (clarified butter). The South Indians and Tamils of Sri Lanka generally use sesame seed, groundnut, coconut and other vegetable oils. The Sri Lankan Singhalese use coconut oil almost exclusively.

The Northern Indians, some South Indians and the Tamils of North Sri Lanka marinate their meats in yogurt, which also acts as a tenderizer. The South Indian Tamils, and the Tamils and Singhalese of Sri Lanka, also use asopfection perunkayam, vinegar, lime, lemon, tamarind, tomatoes, the crushed leaves of papaya or the juice of the raw fruit yielding papein, crushed pomegranate seeds and acid fruits such as young mangoes.

The Northern Indians, especially, are the makers of great stocks. The two classic ones are *akni* or vegetable stock – a court bouillon with a vegetable base and aromatics – and *yakni* or meat stock – a thick double-layered jelly of meat and vegetable stock with aromatics. These they use for the cooking of *pulaus* and *biryanis*. The South Indians and the Sri Lankan Tamils also make tasty stocks or 'soups' which they use as separate dishes within

(Above) Mustard is grown extensively in India and is a basic ingredient for many Indian recipes.

(Right) Women workers gather a rich crop of tea on a plantation in India.

the framework of a balanced meal when, for example, the main meat dish is a dry *korma*. Their *rasam* – coriander soup – and *mulliguthanni* or pepper-water soup (translated into mulligatawny soup by the British) are both famous.

The Northern Indians use cream and yogurt to thicken their sauces and gravies; the South Indians use yogurt and the first thick milk of coconuts, as do the Sri Lankans. However, in addition to their aromatizing effects, *masalas* are also used as thickening agents; as are crushed nuts such as cashewnuts, peanuts, almonds and pistachio nuts; poppy seed and jackfruit and breadfruit seeds powdered or pulverized; raw rice or par boiled rice roasted; fruits such as tomatoes onions and garlic ground into pastes or finely pulverized; green and red chillis, ground; coriander, fenugreek, fennel, dill, mustard, mint, parsley or murunga leaves; chal and other lentils and pulses cooked to a pulp, roasted grated coconut pounded maldive fish or the finely pulverized head and shells of shrimps and prawns for thickening seafood dishes.

In the North of India they powder and pound their spices. In the South and in Sri Lanka the cooking *masalas* are made up of ground spices and usually made up first into wet *masalas* – that is, as

pastes. The spices are ground daily, especially in the South, on a grinding stone using water, saltwater, coconutwater, lime or lemon juice, or tamarind or goraka water, according to the requirements of that day's recipes.

A dry-ground roasted *masala* mix called *garam masala* – for which various people have various recipes they swear by, is used as an aromatic garnish for certain dishes but it must never be treated as a cooking *masala*; it can give the dish a heavy and musty flavour.

Gold and silver foil so thin 'a breath could blow it away', is used both to beautify the dish and to act as a digestive, mostly by the Northern Indians. The Southerners make pretty patterns of the coloured powders of paprika, turmeric, chopped parsleys and spring greens (collards). Most important of all the actual laying out of the food in bowls and dishes should be the greatest appetizer of all: appealing to the 'senses of the eyes' – physical and spiritual!

Feasts of this fare are fun to make once one has learned a little about the cuisine.

Serving Indian Food

Whether one is ordering it in a restaurant or making it oneself the meal must always be balanced, not only from a point of dietary value – a fair balance of proteins, fats and carbohydrates – but from a point of view of texture and flavour. If a dryish *korma* is the main meat dish, the vegetable or fish dish accompanying it must be a gravy curry together with, say, a medium dry lentil dish. The Southerners, especially, consider a meal a success when one of the dishes causes 'the mouth to burn'. They will then 'balance' this with a cooling buttermilk or curd preparation such as a *raita*. They will probably also have a salad or fresh vegetable chutney. (Quite apart from the preserved variety of jam-like chutneys.) They will usually also have some fresh pickles or *achars*, *sambals* (pungent mixtures of meats, fish or vegetables ground finely or pounded together), *cachombars* (fresh mixed vegetables mixed with fresh herbs), fried bombay duck and fried or roasted poppadums and the preserved chutneys.

All the dishes are served at once and it is up to the person eating to serve themselves the meal with the flavours which they wish to predominate. In short, there are two levels of artistry involved: that of the chef and that of the diner. And perhaps even a third: that of the hostess who, once she has cooked her meal, will set it out in such a way and in such proportions, that the guests will be inclined to follow her lead and take the food as she has apportioned it.

A mouth watering selection
of typical Indians breads.

VEGETABLES & PULSE

Turkari Aloo

(Curried Potatoes)

Metric/Imperial	American
50g./2oz. ghee or clarified butter	¼ cup ghee or clarified butter
½ tsp. turmeric	½ tsp. turmeric
700g./1½lb. potatoes, cut into 2½cm./1in. cubes	1½lb. potatoes, cut into 1in. cubes
3 garlic cloves, crushed	3 garlic cloves, crushed
2 green chillis, chopped	2 green chillis, chopped
1 tsp. ground fenugreek	1 tsp. ground fenugreek
1 Tbs. ground coriander	1 Tbs. ground coriander
1 tsp. salt	1 tsp. salt
450ml./15fl.oz. yogurt, well beaten	2 cups yogurt, well beaten
1 Tbs. chopped coriander leaves	1 Tbs. chopped coriander leaves

Melt the ghee or clarified butter in a saucepan. Add the turmeric and potatoes and fry, turning the cubes frequently, until they are lightly and evenly browned. Stir in the garlic, chillis, spices and salt and fry for 3 minutes, stirring constantly. Stir in the yogurt. Bring to the boil, reduce the heat to low and simmer the mixture for 30 minutes, or until the potatoes are tender.

Transfer the mixture to a warmed serving dish, and sprinkle over the coriander before serving.

Serves 4
Preparation and cooking time: 45 minutes

Gobi Ki Sabzi

(Spicy Cauliflower)

Metric/Imperial	American
5 Tbs. vegetable oil	5 Tbs. vegetable oil
1 tsp. mustard seeds	1 tsp. mustard seeds
2½cm./1in. piece of fresh root ginger, peeled and cut into thin strips	1in. piece of fresh green ginger, peeled and cut into thin strips
1 onion, sliced	1 onion, sliced
1 tsp. turmeric	1 tsp. turmeric
1 green chilli, chopped	1 green chilli, chopped
1 large cauliflower, separated into flowerets	1 large cauliflower, separated into flowerets
1 tsp. salt	1 tsp. salt
juice of ½ lemon	juice of ½ lemon
1 Tbs. chopped coriander leaves	1 Tbs. chopped coriander leaves

Heat the oil in a saucepan. When it is hot, add the mustard seeds and cover the

an. When the seeds stop spattering, remove the lid and add the ginger, onion, urmeric and chilli. Fry for 3 minutes, stirring occasionally.

Stir in the cauliflower pieces and salt and sprinkle over the lemon juice. Cover he pan, reduce the heat to low and simmer for 20 minutes, or until the cauliflower s tender.

Transfer the mixture to a warmed serving dish and sprinkle over the coriander efore serving.

erves 4

reparation and cooking time: 35 minutes

Gobi Ki Sabzi is a hot, spicy dish of cauliflower, well seasoned with mustard seeds.

Dum Gobi

(Cauliflower Baked in Yogurt)

Metric/Imperial	American
1 cauliflower, separated into flowerets	1 cauliflower, separated into flowerets
1 onion, finely chopped	1 onion, finely chopped
300ml./10fl.oz. yogurt	1¼ cups yogurt
2 Tbs. tomato purée	2 Tbs. tomato paste
1 tsp. ground coriander	1 tsp. ground coriander
1 tsp. garam masala	1 tsp. garam masala
¼ tsp. ground ginger	¼ tsp. ground ginger
½ tsp. turmeric	½ tsp. turmeric
½ tsp. salt	½ tsp. salt
1 Tbs. ghee or clarified butter, melted	1 Tbs. ghee or clarified butter, melted

Preheat the oven to fairly hot 190°C (Gas Mark 5, 375°F).

Arrange the cauliflower pieces in an ovenproof dish. Blend all the remaining ingredients, except the ghee, together, then pour the mixture over the cauliflower

Put the dish into the oven and bake for 1 hour. Sprinkle the ghee or clarified butter over the cauliflower and return to the oven for a further 1 hour, adding more ghee if the cauliflower becomes too dry.

Transfer to a warmed serving dish and serve at once.

Serves 4
Preparation and cooking time: 2¼ hours

Khutti Dhal

(Spiced Lentils)

Metric/Imperial	American
25g./1oz. ghee or clarified butter	2 Tbs. ghee or clarified butter
1 onion, sliced	1 onion, sliced
1 garlic clove, crushed	1 garlic clove, crushed
1 green chilli, chopped	1 green chilli, chopped
½ tsp. ground cinnamon	½ tsp. ground cinnamon
½ tsp. hot chilli powder	½ tsp. hot chilli powder
225g./8oz. mixed dhal (lentils), washed and drained	1 cup mixed dhal (lentils), washed and drained
725ml./1¼ pints water	3 cups water
½ tsp. salt	½ tsp. salt
250ml./8fl.oz. coconut milk	1 cup coconut milk

Melt the ghee or clarified butter in a saucepan. Add the onion and garlic and fry, stirring occasionally, until the onion is golden brown. Add the chilli and fry for 2 minutes, stirring frequently. Add the cinnamon, chilli powder and dhal (lentils) then pour over the water and salt. Bring to the boil, stirring occasionally. Reduce the heat to low and simmer the mixture for 1 hour, stirring occasionally.

Purée the mixture in a blender, then return to the saucepan. Stir in the coconut milk and bring to the boil. Simmer for 10 minutes.

Transfer the mixture to a warmed serving bowl and serve at once.

Serves 4

Preparation and cooking time: 1½ hours

Sambar

(Lentils Cooked with Spices)

Metric/Imperial	American
225g./8oz. toovar dhal (lentils), soaked in cold water for 1 hour and drained	1 cup toovar dhal (lentils), soaked in cold water for 1 hour and drained
¼ tsp. ground fenugreek	¼ tsp. ground fenugreek
1¼l./2 pints water	5 cups water
1½ tsp. salt	1½ tsp. salt
50g./2oz. fresh coconut, chopped	⅓ cup chopped fresh coconut,
2 tsp. cumin seeds	2 tsp. cumin seeds
1 Tbs. coriander seeds	1 Tbs. coriander seeds
½ tsp. ground cinnamon	½ tsp. ground cinnamon
50g./2oz. tamarind	¼ cup tamarind
250ml./8fl.oz. boiling water	1 cup boiling water
2 tsp. soft brown sugar	2 tsp. soft brown sugar
1 tsp. hot chilli powder	1 tsp. hot chilli powder
2 Tbs. chopped coriander leaves	2 Tbs. chopped coriander leaves
2 Tbs. vegetable oil	2 Tbs. vegetable oil
1 tsp. mustard seeds	1 tsp. mustard seeds
1 tsp. turmeric	1 tsp. turmeric
¼ tsp. asafoetida	¼ tsp. asafoetida
2 garlic cloves, crushed	2 garlic cloves, crushed
1 green chilli, finely chopped	1 green chilli, finely chopped

Put the dhal, fenugreek, water and 1 teaspoon of salt into a saucepan and bring to the boil. Reduce the heat to low and simmer for 1 hour, or until the dhal is soft. Remove from the heat.

Meanwhile, cook the coconut, cumin, coriander and cinnamon in a frying-pan for 3 minutes, stirring constantly. Remove from the heat and cool. Purée the mixture in a blender with 4 tablespoons of water. Transfer to a bowl and set aside.

Put the tamarind into a bowl and pour over the water. Set aside until it is cool. Pour the contents of the bowl through a strainer into a saucepan, pressing as much of the pulp through as possible. Put the saucepan over moderate heat and stir in the sugar, chilli powder, coriander leaves and remaining salt. Simmer for 5 minutes. Remove from the heat and set aside.

Heat the oil in a small frying-pan. Add the mustard seeds and cover. When they begin to spatter, stir in the remaining spices, garlic and chilli. Reduce the heat to low and fry for 2 minutes, stirring constantly. Spoon the contents of the pan into the dhal with the tamarind mixture and coconut and spice purée. Stir to mix. Return the pan to low heat and simmer for 10 minutes, stirring frequently.

Transfer the mixture to a warmed serving bowl and serve at once.

Serves 4-6

Preparation and cooking time: 3 hours

(See over) Sambar, a dish originating from South India, is often served with boiled rice as part of an Indian meal.

15

Ekuri

(Scrambled Eggs with Chilli)
This is one of the specialities of the Parsees, a religious community on the west coast of India.

Metric/Imperial	American
40g./1½oz. butter	3 Tbs. butter
1 medium onion, chopped	1 medium onion, chopped
1cm./½in. piece of fresh root ginger, peeled and chopped	½in. piece of fresh green ginger, peeled and chopped
1 green chilli, chopped	1 green chilli, chopped
½ tsp. turmeric	½ tsp. turmeric
2 Tbs. chopped coriander leaves	2 Tbs. chopped coriander leaves
½ tsp. salt	½ tsp. salt
8 eggs, lightly beaten	8 eggs, lightly beaten
4 slices toast	4 slices toast
2 tomatoes, quartered	2 tomatoes, quartered

Melt the butter in a frying-pan. Add the onion and ginger and fry, stirring occasionally, until the onion is golden brown. Stir in the chilli, turmeric, 1½ tablespoons of coriander and the salt, and fry for 1 minute. Pour in the eggs, reduce the heat to low and cook the eggs until they are softly scrambled, stirring constantly.

Spoon the mixture on to the toast slices and garnish with the tomatoes and remaining coriander before serving.
Serves 4
Preparation and cooking time: 15 minutes

Mattar Pannir

(Peas and Cheese)

Metric/Imperial	American
50g./2oz. ghee or clarified butter	¼ cup ghee or clarified butter
4cm./1½in. piece of fresh root ginger, peeled and chopped	1½in. piece of fresh green ginger, peeled and chopped
2 garlic cloves, crushed	2 garlic cloves, crushed
1½ tsp. coriander seeds	1½ tsp. coriander seeds
½ tsp. cardamom seeds	½ tsp. cardamom seeds
½ tsp. hot chilli powder	½ tsp. hot chilli powder
1 tsp. turmeric	1 tsp. turmeric
½kg./1lb. peas, weighed after shelling	2⅔ cups peas, weighed after shelling
350g./12oz. feta or goat cheese	12oz. feta or goat cheese
3 tomatoes, blanched, peeled and chopped	3 tomatoes, blanched, peeled and chopped
1 Tbs. chopped coriander leaves	1 Tbs. chopped coriander leaves

Melt the ghee or clarified butter in a saucepan. Add the ginger and garlic and fry for 3 minutes, stirring constantly. Stir in the coriander and spices and fry for a further 1 minute, stirring constantly. Add a spoonful or two of water if the mixture becomes too dry. Stir in the peas and simmer for 10 minutes. Stir in the

...eese and tomatoes and simmer for a further 10 minutes.

Transfer to a warmed serving dish and sprinkle over the coriander before ...rving.

...rves 6

...reparation and cooking time: 35 minutes

Tamatar Bharta

(...ureéd Tomatoes)

Metric/Imperial	American
...0g./1½lb. tomatoes	1½lb. tomatoes
...Tbs. vegetable oil	2 Tbs. vegetable oil
...medium onions, chopped	2 medium onions, chopped
...green chillis, chopped	2 green chillis, chopped
...m./½in. piece of fresh root ginger, peeled and chopped	½in. piece of fresh green ginger, peeled and chopped
...tsp. salt	1 tsp. salt
...tsp. sugar	1 tsp. sugar
...Tbs. yogurt	5 Tbs. yogurt
...Tbs. chopped coriander leaves	1 Tbs. chopped coriander leaves

...lanch, peel and chop the tomatoes finely or, for a better flavour, put them under ...hot grill (broiler) until the skins are scorched, then peel and chop them. Set ...ide.

Heat the oil in a saucepan. When it is hot, add the onions, chillis and ginger ...d fry, stirring frequently, until the onions are golden brown. Stir in the salt, ...gar, yogurt and tomatoes and simmer, stirring occasionally, for 30 minutes, or ...til the mixture is thick.

Transfer the mixture to a warmed serving bowl and sprinkle over the coriander ...efore serving.

...rves 4

...reparation and cooking time: 1 hour

Vendai Kai Kari

(...urried Okra)

Metric/Imperial	American
...0g./2oz. tamarind	¼ cup tamarind
...50ml./8fl.oz. boiling water	1 cup boiling water
...Tbs. vegetable oil	5 Tbs. vegetable oil
...0g./1½lb. okra, sliced	1½lb. okra, sliced
...medium onions, sliced	2 medium onions, sliced
...cm./1in. piece of fresh root ginger, peeled and chopped	1in. piece of fresh green ginger, peeled and chopped
...garlic cloves, crushed	2 garlic cloves, crushed
...green chillis, sliced	2 green chillis, sliced

1 tsp. turmeric	1 tsp. turmeric
1 Tbs. ground coriander	1 Tbs. ground coriander
250ml./8fl.oz. coconut milk	1 cup coconut milk
1 tsp. salt	1 tsp. salt
1 tsp. mustard seeds	1 tsp. mustard seeds
4 curry or bay leaves	4 curry or bay leaves

Put the tamarind in a small bowl. Pour over the boiling water and set aside unt
it is cool. Pour the contents of the bowl through a strainer, pressing as much c
the pulp through as possible.

Heat 4 tablespoons of the oil in a saucepan. When it is hot, add the okra an
fry, stirring occasionally, until it is evenly browned. Using a slotted spoor
transfer the okra to a plate and set aside. Add the onions, ginger, garlic an
chillis to the pan and fry, stirring occasionally, until the onions are golde
brown. Stir in the spices and fry for 3 minutes, stirring constantly. Add a spoonf
or two of water if the mixture becomes too dry.

Stir in the tamarind juice, return the okra to the pan and bring to the boi
Cover the pan, reduce the heat to low and simmer for 5 minutes. Stir in th
coconut milk and salt and bring to the boil again. Reduce the heat to low agai
and simmer for 10 minutes.

Meanwhile, heat the remaining oil in a small frying-pan. When it is hot, ad
the mustard seeds and curry or bay leaves. Cover, and when the seeds sto
spattering, stir the mixture into the okra mixture. Cook for 1 minute.

Transfer to a warmed serving dish and serve at once.
Serves 4
Preparation and cooking time: 1 hour

Khichri

(Rice with Lentils)

Metric/Imperial	American
65g./2½oz. butter	5 Tbs. butter
1 onion, finely chopped	1 onion, finely chopped
2½cm./1in. piece of fresh root ginger, peeled and chopped	1in. piece of fresh green ginger, peeled and chopped
1 garlic clove, crushed	1 garlic clove, crushed
6 peppercorns	6 peppercorns
1 bay leaf	1 bay leaf
225g./8oz. long-grain rice and 125g./4oz. yellow moong dhal (lentils), soaked together in cold water for 1 hour and drained	1⅓ cups long-grain rice and ½ cup yellow moong dhal (lentils), soaked together in cold water for 1 hour and drained
1 tsp. salt	1 tsp. salt
½ tsp. turmeric	½ tsp. turmeric
600ml./1 pint boiling water	2½ cups boiling water
fried onion slices	fried onion slices

Melt 40g./1½oz. (3 tablespoons) of the butter in a saucepan. Add the onion an
fry, stirring occasionally, until it is soft. Stir in the ginger, garlic, peppercorns an
bay leaf and fry for 3 minutes, stirring constantly. Add the rice, dhal, salt an
turmeric and stir well. Simmer for 5 minutes, stirring frequently.

Pour in the water and stir once. Cover the pan, reduce the heat to low an
simmer for 15 to 20 minutes, or until the rice is cooked and the liquid is absorbe
Stir in the remaining butter.

Transfer the mixture to a warmed serving dish, scatter over the fried onions and serve at once.

Serves 4
Preparation and cooking time: 1½ hours

Vegetable kitcheri

Metric/Imperial	American
2 tsp. salt	2 tsp. salt
225g./8oz. long-grain rice, soaked in cold water for 30 minutes and drained	1⅓ cups long-grain rice, soaked in cold water for 30 minutes and drained
75g./3oz. moong dhal (lentils), washed and drained	⅓ cup moong dhal (lentils), washed and drained
50g./2oz. tur dhal, washed and drained	¼ cup tur dhal, washed and drained
75g./3oz. masoor dhal, washed and drained	⅓ cup masoor dhal, washed and drained
65g./2½oz. butter	5 Tbs. butter
2 medium onions, sliced	2 medium onions, sliced
2 green chillis, chopped	2 green chillis, chopped
2½cm./1in. piece of fresh root ginger, peeled and chopped	1in. piece of fresh green ginger, peeled and chopped
2 garlic cloves, crushed	2 garlic cloves, crushed
1 Tbs. ground coriander	1 Tbs. ground coriander
½ tsp. turmeric	½ tsp. turmeric
1 potato, cubed	1 potato, cubed
1 large carrot, cubed	1 large carrot, cubed
1 small aubergine, cubed	1 small eggplant, cubed
125g./4oz. peas, weighed after shelling	⅔ cup peas, weighed after shelling
½ small cauliflower, separated into flowerets	½ small cauliflower, separated into flowerets
2 large tomatoes, blanched, peeled and chopped	2 large tomatoes, blanched, peeled and chopped
450ml./15fl.oz. chicken stock	2 cups chicken stock
25 g./1oz. butter, melted	2 Tbs. butter, melted

Half-fill a saucepan with boiling water and stir in ½ teaspoon of salt. Add the rice, bring to the boil again and boil the rice for 3 minutes. Remove from the heat and drain the rice. Set aside. Half-fill the same saucepan with boiling water again and stir in another ½ teaspoon of salt. Add the dhals (lentils), bring to the boil and boil for 5 minutes. Remove from the heat and drain the dhals. Set aside.

Melt 50g./2oz. (4 tablespoons) of the butter in a large frying-pan. Add the onions and fry, stirring occasionally, until they are golden brown. Add the chillis, ginger and garlic and fry for 2 minutes, stirring frequently. Stir in the coriander and turmeric and fry for 1 minute. Add the vegetables and remaining salt and stir well. Cover the pan, reduce the heat to moderately low and simmer for 20 to 30 minutes, or until the vegetables are tender.

Preheat the oven to very cool 140°C (Gas Mark 1, 275°F). Use the remaining butter to grease a large flameproof casserole. Make layers of the dhals, vegetables and rice in the casserole, in that order, ending with a layer of rice. Pour in the stock and cook the mixture for 1 minute. Cover and transfer to the oven. Cook for 45 minutes to 1 hour, or until the dhals and rice are cooked and the liquid is absorbed.

Remove from the oven, sprinkle over the melted butter and serve, straight from the dish.

Serves 6
Preparation and cooking time: 2½ hours

(See over) Vegetable Kitcheri, an imaginative mixture of rice and assorted vegetables, is a delicious and substantial vegetarian dish.

Wengi Bhat and Wengyachen Bharit are tasty Indian vegetable dishes, with aubergines (eggplants) as their main ingredient.

Wengyachen Bharit

(Curried Aubergines [Eggplants])

Metric/Imperial	American
1kg./2lb. aubergines	2lb. eggplants
40g./1½oz. butter	3 Tbs. butter
3 medium onions, chopped	3 medium onions, chopped
4 garlic cloves, crushed	4 garlic cloves, crushed
5cm./2in. piece of fresh root ginger, peeled and chopped	2in. piece of fresh green ginger, peeled and chopped
2 green chillis, seeded and chopped	2 green chillis, seeded and chopped
½ bunch chopped coriander leaves	½ bunch chopped coriander leaves
1 tsp. turmeric	1 tsp. turmeric

1 tsp. ground cumin	1 tsp. ground cumin
1 tsp. salt	1 tsp. salt
175ml./6fl.oz. yogurt	¾ cup yogurt
2 tsp. sugar	2 tsp. sugar

Preheat the oven to moderate 180°C (Gas Mark 4, 350°F).

Make three cuts in each aubergine (eggplant) and arrange on a baking sheet. Put the sheet into the oven and bake the aubergines (eggplants) for 45 minutes to 1 hour, or until they are soft. Remove from the oven and set aside until they are cool enough to handle. Peel and discard the skins and transfer the pulp to a bowl. Mash to a smooth purée.

Melt the butter in a saucepan. Add the onions and fry, stirring occasionally, until they are golden brown. Stir in the garlic, ginger and chillis and fry for 3 minutes, stirring frequently. Stir in the coriander, turmeric and cumin. Cook for 1 minute. Add the aubergine (eggplant) purée and salt and cook for 5 minutes, stirring frequently.

Stir in the yogurt and sugar, then transfer to a warmed serving dish and serve at once.

Serves 4
Preparation and cooking time: 2 hours

Wengi Bhat

(Aubergines [Eggplants] and Rice)

Metric/Imperial	American
6 small aubergines	6 small eggplants
2 dried red chillis	2 dried red chillis
2 garlic cloves	2 garlic cloves
1 tsp. mustard seeds	1 tsp. mustard seeds
1 tsp. turmeric	1 tsp. turmeric
4 cloves	4 cloves
6 black peppercorns	6 black peppercorns
1 tsp. cumin seeds	1 tsp. cumin seeds
1 tsp. white poppy seeds	1 tsp. white poppy seeds
3 Tbs. peanuts	3 Tbs. peanuts
4-6 Tbs. water	4-6 Tbs. water
75g./3oz. butter	6 Tbs. butter
1½ tsp. salt	1½ tsp. salt
2 medium onions, sliced	2 medium onions, sliced
350g./12oz. long-grain rice, soaked in cold water for 30 minutes and drained	2 cups long-grain rice, soaked in cold water for 30 minutes and drained
2 Tbs. desiccated coconut, blended with 2 Tbs. water	2 Tbs. shredded coconut, blended with 2 Tbs. water

Cut the aubergines (eggplants) in half, lengthways, and scoop out the flesh. Reserve the skins. Put the pulp in a bowl.

Blend the spices, peanuts and water to a smooth purée, adding the extra water if necessary. Transfer the purée to a small bowl.

Melt 25g./1oz. (2 tablespoons) of butter in a frying-pan. Add the spice purée and fry for 3 minutes, stirring constantly. Stir in the aubergine (eggplant) pulp and half the salt and fry for 7 minutes, stirring frequently. Spoon the mixture into the reserved skins and set aside.

Rinse and dry the frying-pan. Melt a further 25g./1oz. (2 tablespoons) of butter in the pan. Add the onions and fry, stirring occasionally, until they are golden brown. Add the stuffed aubergines (eggplants), reduce the heat to low and simmer for 5 minutes. Remove from the heat.

Preheat the oven to cool 150°C (Gas Mark 2, 300°F).

Melt the remaining butter in a saucepan. Add the rice and remaining salt and fry for 3 minutes, stirring constantly. Pour in enough boiling water to cover the rice by 1cm./½in. and bring to the boil. Cover the pan, reduce the heat to low and simmer for 15 to 20 minutes, or until the rice is cooked and the liquid is absorbed. Remove from the heat and stir in the coconut.

Arrange a third of the rice in a large baking dish and cover with half the aubergine (eggplant) halves, cut sides uppermost. Continue making layers in this way, ending with a layer of rice. Cover and put the dish into the oven. Bake for 25 minutes.

Remove from the oven and serve at once, from the dish.

Serves 4-6
Preparation and cooking time: 2 hours

Kabli Channa

(Whole Chick-Peas)

Metric/Imperial	American
225g./8oz. dried chick-peas, soaked overnight and drained	1⅓ cups dried chick-peas, soaked overnight and drained
600ml./1 pint water	2½ cups water
1 tsp. salt	1 tsp. salt
50ml./2fl.oz. vegetable oil	¼ cup vegetable oil
2 medium onions, sliced	2 medium onions, sliced
2 garlic cloves, chopped	2 garlic cloves, chopped
2½cm./1in. piece of fresh root ginger, peeled and cut into thin strips	1in. piece of fresh green ginger, peeled and cut into thin strips
1 tsp. turmeric	1 tsp. turmeric
1 tsp. ground cumin	1 tsp. ground cumin
2 tsp. ground coriander	2 tsp. ground coriander
4 green chillis, slit open	4 green chillis, slit open
1 large tomato, blanched, peeled, seeded and chopped	1 large tomato, blanched, peeled, seeded and chopped
1 green pepper, pith and seeds removed and cut into strips	1 green pepper, pith and seeds removed and cut into strips
juice of 1½ lemons	juice of 1½ lemons
1 tsp. garam masala	1 tsp. garam masala
2 Tbs. chopped coriander leaves	2 Tbs. chopped coriander leaves

Put the chick-peas into a saucepan and add the water and ¼ teaspoon of salt. Bring to the boil, cover and reduce the heat to low. Simmer for 1½ hours, or until the peas are tender. Drain and reserve 300ml./10fl.oz. (1¼ cups) of the cooking liquid.

Heat the oil in a frying-pan.

When it is hot, add the onions and garlic and fry, stirring occasionally, until the onions are golden brown. Add the ginger and fry for 1 minute, then stir in the spices and fry for 5 minutes, stirring constantly. Add a spoonful or two of water if the mixture becomes too dry. Add the chillis, tomato and pepper and cook for 5 minutes. Stir in the chick-peas and cook for a further 7 minutes. Stir in the reserved cooking liquid, the remaining salt and the lemon juice, and bring to the boil.

Cover the frying-pan and reduce the heat to low. Simmer for 15 minutes, uncover and simmer for a further 10 minutes.

Transfer the mixture to a warmed serving dish and sprinkle over the garam masala and coriander before serving.

Serves 4
Preparation and cooking time: 2¼ hours

Sabzi Pulao

(Vegetable Pilaff)

Metric/Imperial	American
125g./4oz. butter	8 Tbs. butter
1 medium onion, sliced	1 medium onion, sliced

2 garlic cloves, crushed

2½cm./1in. piece of fresh root ginger, peeled and chopped

1 green chilli, seeded and chopped

1 tsp. turmeric

½ tsp. hot chilli powder

225g./8oz. cauliflower, separated into flowerets

125g./4oz. peas, weighed after shelling

125g./4oz. carrots, sliced

1 small aubergine, cubed

1 small green pepper, pith and seeds removed and chopped

2 potatoes, cubed

2 tomatoes, blanched, peeled and chopped

175ml./6fl.oz. chicken stock

1 Tbs. chopped coriander leaves

1 tsp. salt

350g./12oz. long-grain rice, cooked until just tender

2 garlic cloves, crushed

1in. piece of fresh green ginger, peeled and chopped

1 green chilli, seeded and chopped

1 tsp. turmeric

½ tsp. hot chilli powder

8oz. cauliflower, separated into flowerets

⅔ cup peas, weighed after shelling

⅔ cup sliced carrots

1 small eggplant, cubed

1 small green pepper, pith and seeds removed and chopped

2 potatoes, cubed

2 tomatoes, blanched, peeled and chopped

¾ cup chicken stock

1 Tbs. chopped coriander leaves

1 tsp. salt

2 cups long-grain rice, cooked until just tender

Aviyal, a versatile curry, can be made from any combination of vegetables.

28

GARNISH
1 Tbs. butter
2 Tbs. slivered almonds
2 Tbs. raisins

GARNISH
1 Tbs. butter
2 Tbs. slivered almonds
2 Tbs. raisins

Melt the butter in a frying-pan. Add the onion, garlic, ginger and chilli and fry, stirring occasionally, until the onion is golden brown. Stir in the turmeric and chilli powder and fry for 1 minute, stirring constantly. Add the remaining vegetables, one at a time, stirring well before adding the next. Pour in the stock and bring to the boil. Stir in the coriander and salt, cover and reduce the heat to low. Simmer for 25 to 30 minutes, or until the vegetables are tender. Remove from the heat.

Preheat the oven to warm 170°C (Gas Mark 3, 325°F). Layer the rice and vegetable mixture in a well-greased baking dish, beginning and ending with a layer of rice. Cover and put the dish into the oven. Bake for 25 minutes.

Meanwhile, to prepare the garnish, melt the butter in a frying-pan. Add the almonds and raisins and fry, stirring constantly, until they are lightly browned. Remove from the heat.

Remove the dish from the oven and scatter over the garnish before serving.
Serves 6
Preparation and cooking time: 1½ hours

Aviyal

(Vegetable Curry)

You can use any combination of vegetables you wish in this spicy dish – carrots, beans, aubergine (eggplant), turnip, cauliflower, green pepper, potatoes and spring onions (scallions) were used in the version photographed.

Metric/Imperial	American
50ml./2fl.oz. vegetable oil	¼ cup vegetable oil
1 tsp. mustard seeds	1 tsp. mustard seeds
5cm./2in. piece of fresh root ginger, peeled and minced	2in. piece of fresh green ginger, peeled and ground
2 garlic cloves, quartered	2 garlic cloves, quartered
1 onion, grated	1 onion, grated
1 green chilli, minced	1 green chilli, ground
1½ tsp. turmeric	1½ tsp. turmeric
1 Tbs. ground coriander	1 Tbs. ground coriander
700g./1½lb. mixed vegetables, sliced	1½lb. mixed vegetables, sliced
1 tsp. salt	1 tsp. salt
225g./8oz. fresh coconut or 2½cm./1in. slice creamed coconut, puréed with 175ml./6fl.oz. water.	8oz. fresh coconut or 1in. slice creamed coconut, puréed with ¾ cup water
2 Tbs. chopped coriander leaves	2 Tbs. chopped coriander leaves

Heat the oil in a large saucepan. When it is hot, add the mustard seeds, ginger and garlic and fry for 30 seconds, stirring constantly. Add the onion and chilli and fry until the onion is golden brown. Stir in the turmeric and coriander and cook for 1 minute. Add the vegetables and stir to mix. Stir in the salt and coconut purée. Add a spoonful or two of water if the mixture becomes too dry. Cover the pan and simmer for 30 minutes, or until the vegetables are tender.

Transfer the mixture to a warmed serving dish and sprinkle over the chopped coriander before serving.
Serves 4
Preparation and cooking time: 40 minutes

MEAT

Kheema

(Curried Minced [Ground] Lamb)

Metric/Imperial	American
50ml./2fl.oz. vegetable oil	¼ cup vegetable oil
3 large onions, sliced	3 large onions, sliced
2½cm./1in. piece of fresh root ginger, peeled and chopped	1in. piece of fresh green ginger, peeled and chopped
2 garlic cloves, crushed	2 garlic cloves, crushed
1 tsp. turmeric	1 tsp. turmeric
1 tsp. hot chilli powder	1 tsp. hot chilli powder
1 tsp. ground coriander	1 tsp. ground coriander
700g./1½lb. minced lamb	1½lb. ground lamb
1 tsp. salt	1 tsp. salt
3 tomatoes, blanched, peeled, seeded and chopped	3 tomatoes, blanched, peeled, seeded and chopped
2 Tbs. chopped coriander leaves	2 Tbs. chopped coriander leaves

Heat the oil in a deep frying-pan. When it is hot, add the onions, ginger and garlic and fry, stirring occasionally, until the onions are soft. Stir in the spices and fry for 3 minutes, stirring frequently. Add the meat and fry until it loses its pinkness. Stir in the salt and tomatoes and bring to the boil. Cover the pan, reduce the heat to low and simmer for 15 minutes. Uncover and simmer for a further 5 minutes, or until the meat is cooked through.

Transfer the mixture to a warmed serving dish and sprinkle over the coriander before serving.
Serves 4
Preparation and cooking time: 35 minutes

Roghan Gosht

(Curried Lamb)

Metric/Imperial	American
250ml./8fl.oz. yogurt	1 cup yogurt
¼ tsp. asafoetida	¼ tsp. asafoetida
½ tsp. cayenne pepper	½ tsp. cayenne pepper
1kg./2lb. lean lamb, cubed	2lb. lean lamb, cubed
4cm./1½in. piece of fresh root ginger, peeled and chopped	1½in. piece of fresh green ginger, peeled and chopped
4 garlic cloves	4 garlic cloves
1 tsp. white poppy seeds	1 tsp. white poppy seeds
1 tsp. cumin seeds	1 tsp. cumin seeds
1 Tbs. coriander seeds	1 Tbs. coriander seeds
4 cloves	4 cloves
2 Tbs. cardamom seeds	2 Tbs. cardamom seeds
8 peppercorns	8 peppercorns

2 Tbs. unblanched almonds	2 Tbs. unblanched almonds
50g./2oz. ghee or clarified butter	4 Tbs. ghee or clarified butter
1 medium onion, chopped	1 medium onion, chopped
1 tsp. turmeric	1 tsp. turmeric
250ml./8fl.oz. water	1 cup water
1 tsp. garam masala	1 tsp. garam masala
1 Tbs. chopped coriander leaves	1 Tbs. chopped coriander leaves

Roghan Gosht is a delicately flavoured lamb curry and very popular among the inhabitants of North India.

Combine the yogurt, asafoetida and cayenne in a large bowl and stir in the meat cubes. Cover and set aside.

Put the ginger, garlic, spices and almonds in a blender with 4 tablespoons of water and blend to a smooth purée. Transfer to a small bowl.

Melt the ghee or clarified butter in a flameproof casserole. Add the onion and fry, stirring occasionally, until it is golden brown. Stir in the turmeric and spice purée and fry for 8 minutes, stirring constantly. Add a spoonful or two of water if the mixture becomes too dry. Add the lamb cubes and yogurt mixture and fry until the cubes are evenly browned. Cover the casserole, reduce the heat to low and simmer for 45 minutes.

Preheat the oven to very cool 140°C (Gas Mark 1, 275°F).

Uncover the casserole and stir in 50ml./2fl.oz. (¼ cup) of water. Add another 50ml./2fl.oz. (¼ cup) of water and stir until it has been absorbed. Pour in the remaining water, cover the casserole and reduce the heat to low. Simmer for a further 15 minutes.

Stir in the garam masala and coriander leaves. Cover the casserole and put it into the oven. Cook for 25 minutes.

Transfer the mixture to a warmed serving dish and serve at once.

Serves 4-6
Preparation and cooking time: 1¾ hours

Lamb and Cashew Nut Curry can be served either with rice or chapattis and makes a substantial meal.

Lamb and Cashew Nut Curry

Metric/Imperial	American
4cm./1½in. piece of fresh root ginger, peeled and chopped	1½in. piece of fresh green ginger, peeled and chopped
3 garlic cloves	3 garlic cloves
2 green chillis	2 green chillis
50g./2oz. unsalted cashewnuts	½ cup unsalted cashewnuts
50-75ml./2-3fl.oz. water	¼-⅓ cup water
4 cloves	4 cloves
¼ tsp. cardamom seeds	¼ tsp. cardamom seeds
1 Tbs. coriander seeds	1 Tbs. coriander seeds
1 Tbs. white poppy seeds	1 Tbs. white poppy seeds
50g./2oz. butter	4 Tbs. butter
2 onions, finely chopped	2 onions, finely chopped
1kg./2lb. lean lamb, cubed	2lb. lean lamb, cubed
300ml./10fl.oz. yogurt	1¼ cups yogurt
¼ tsp. saffron threads, soaked in 2 Tbs. boiling water	¼ tsp. saffron threads, soaked in 2 Tbs. boiling water
1 tsp. salt	1 tsp. salt
juice of ¼ lemon	juice of ¼ lemon
1 Tbs. chopped coriander leaves	1 Tbs. chopped coriander leaves
1 lemon, sliced	1 lemon, sliced

Put the ginger, garlic, chillis, cashewnuts and half the water in a blender and blend to a smooth purée. Add the cloves, cardamom, coriander and poppy seeds, and enough of the remaining water to prevent the blender from sticking, and blend. Transfer the purée to a bowl.

Melt the butter in a large saucepan. Add the onions and fry, stirring occasionally, until they are golden brown. Stir in the spice purée and fry for 3 minutes, stirring constantly. Add the lamb cubes and fry until they are evenly browned.

Beat the yogurt with the saffron and salt, then stir the mixture into the pan. Bring to the boil, reduce the heat to low and simmer the curry for 1 hour. Stir in the lemon juice and sprinkle over the coriander. Cover and simmer for a further 20 minutes, or until the lamb is cooked through and tender.

Serve at once, garnished with the lemon slices.

Serves 4-6
Preparation and cooking time: 1½ hours

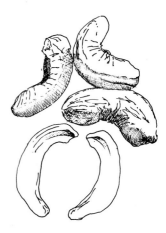

Talawa Gosht

(Deep-Fried Lamb and Potatoes)

Metric/Imperial	American
25g./1oz. butter	2 Tbs. butter
4cm./1½in. piece of fresh root ginger, peeled and chopped	1½in. piece of fresh green ginger, peeled and chopped
3 garlic cloves, crushed	3 garlic cloves, crushed
700g./1½lb. lean lamb, cubed	1½lb. lean lamb, cubed
1 tsp. turmeric	1 tsp. turmeric
2 tsp. hot chilli powder	2 tsp. hot chilli powder
½ tsp. salt	½ tsp. salt
50ml./2fl.oz. yogurt	¼ cup yogurt
vegetable oil for deep-frying	vegetable oil for deep-frying
½kg./1lb. potatoes, boiled until nearly tender, drained and cubed	1lb. potatoes, boiled until nearly tender, drained and cubed
2 lemons, cut into wedges	2 lemons, cut into wedges
BATTER	BATTER
225g./8oz. besan or chick-pea flour	2 cups besan or chick-pea flour
1 tsp. salt	1 tsp. salt
½ tsp. hot chilli powder	½ tsp. hot chilli powder
75ml./3fl.oz. yogurt	⅓ cup yogurt
250ml./8fl.oz. water	1 cup water

Melt the butter in a deep frying-pan. Add the ginger and garlic and fry for 3 minutes, stirring frequently. Add the meat cubes and fry until they are evenly browned.

Meanwhile, combine the spices and yogurt in a small bowl. Stir into the pan and cook, uncovered, for 40 minutes, or until the lamb is just cooked through. Set aside to cool.

To make the batter, sift the flour, salt and chilli powder into a large bowl. Beat in the yogurt and stir in the water, a little at a time, until the mixture forms a smooth batter. Set aside for 30 minutes.

Fill a deep-frying pan one-third full with oil and heat until it is hot. Dip the lamb and potato cubes into the batter, then carefully lower them, a few at a time, into the hot oil. Fry for 3 to 4 minutes, or until they are golden brown and crisp. Drain on kitchen towels.

Serve at once, garnished with lemon wedges.

Serves 4
Preparation and cooking time: 1¼ hours

Huseini Kabab

(Marinated Lamb on Skewers)

Metric/Imperial	American
150ml./5fl.oz. yogurt	⅔ cup yogurt
2 green chillis	2 green chillis
4cm./1½in. piece of fresh root ginger, peeled and chopped	1½in. piece of fresh green ginger, peeled and chopped
1 onion, quartered	1 onion, quartered
1 Tbs. chopped coriander leaves	1 Tbs. chopped coriander leaves
3 garlic cloves	3 garlic cloves
1 tsp. turmeric	1 tsp. turmeric
1 tsp. salt	1 tsp. salt
1kg./2lb. lean lamb, cubed	2lb. lean lamb, cubed
1 tsp. garam masala	1 tsp. garam masala

Put the yogurt, chillis, ginger, onion, coriander, garlic, turmeric and salt into a blender and blend to a smooth purée. Transfer to a large bowl. Stir in the lamb cubes to coat them thoroughly. Cover the bowl and chill in the refrigerator for 6 hours. Remove from the refrigerator and toss and turn the cubes in the marinade. Thread the cubes on to skewers and discard the marinade.

Preheat the grill (broiler) to high.

Arrange the skewers on the grill (broiler) rack and grill (broil) for 10 minutes, turning occasionally, or until the kebabs are cooked through.

Slide the cubes off the skewers on to a warmed serving dish and sprinkle over the garam masala before serving.

Serves 4-6
Preparation and cooking time: 6½ hours

A mildly spiced dish, Tikka Kabab is delicious served with chapattis and various chutneys.

Tikka Kabab

(Spiced Lamb Kebabs)

Metric/Imperial	American
10cm./4in. piece of fresh root ginger, peeled and chopped	4in. piece of fresh green ginger, peeled and chopped
3 medium onions, chopped	3 medium onions, chopped
1 small bunch coriander leaves	1 small bunch coriander leaves
1 Tbs. coriander seeds	1 Tbs. coriander seeds
juice of 1 lemon	juice of 1 lemon
2 green chillis	2 green chillis
½ tsp. black peppercorns	½ tsp. black peppercorns
1kg./2lb. lean lamb, cubed	2 lb. lean lamb, cubed
1 tsp. salt	1 tsp. salt
25g./1oz. butter, melted	2 Tbs. butter, melted

Put the ginger, onions, coriander leaves and seeds, lemon juice, chillis and peppercorns into a blender and blend to a smooth purée. Transfer the puree to a large bowl and stir in the lamb cubes. Cover and set aside at room temperature for 4 hours.

Preheat the grill (broiler) to high. Thread the meat on to skewers and sprinkle over the salt and melted butter. Arrange the skewers on a lined grill (broiler) pan and grill (broil) for 10 to 12 minutes, turning occasionally, or until the cubes are cooked through.

Slide the meat off the skewers on to a warmed serving dish and serve at once.
Serves 4-6
Preparation and cooking time: $4\frac{1}{4}$ hours

Thayir Kari

Metric/Imperial	American
4 garlic cloves	4 garlic cloves
5cm./2in. piece of fresh root ginger, peeled and chopped	2in. piece of fresh green ginger, peeled and chopped
2 green chillis, chopped	2 green chillis, chopped
6 Tbs. chopped coriander leaves	6 Tbs. chopped coriander leaves
$1\frac{1}{2}$ tsp. turmeric	$1\frac{1}{2}$ tsp. turmeric
1 tsp. salt	1 tsp. salt
50ml./2fl.oz. lemon juice	$\frac{1}{4}$ cup lemon juice
1kg./2lb. lean lamb, cubed	2lb. lean lamb, cubed
50ml./2fl.oz. vegetable oil	$\frac{1}{4}$ cup vegetable oil
2 medium onions, chopped	2 medium onions, chopped
600ml./1 pint yogurt	$2\frac{1}{2}$ cups yogurt
$1\frac{1}{2}$ tsp. aniseed, toasted	$1\frac{1}{2}$ tsp. aniseed, toasted

Put the garlic, ginger, chillis, coriander leaves, turmeric and salt into a blender with the lemon juice and blend to a smooth purée. Transfer the purée to a large bowl and stir in the lamb cubes. Set aside at room temperature for 1 hour.

Heat the oil in a large saucepan. When it is hot, add the onions and fry, stirring occasionally, until they are golden brown. Add the lamb cubes and spice purée and fry until the cubes are evenly browned. Stir the yogurt into the lamb mixture and add the aniseed. Bring to the boil, cover the pan and reduce the heat to low. Simmer for $1\frac{1}{4}$ hours, or until the lamb is cooked through and tender. Cook uncovered for the last 20 minutes.

Transfer the curry to a warmed serving bowl and serve at once.
Serves 4-6
Preparation and cooking time: $2\frac{1}{2}$ hours

Shakooti Rassa

(Lamb Cooked with Coconut)

Metric/Imperial	American
6 green chillis, seeded	6 green chillis, seeded
6 Tbs. chopped coriander leaves	6 Tbs. chopped coriander leaves
3 garlic cloves	3 garlic cloves
5cm./2in. piece of fresh root ginger, peeled and chopped	2in. piece of fresh green ginger, peeled and chopped

1 tsp. salt
450ml./15fl.oz. thick coconut milk
1kg./2lb. lean lamb, cubed
5 Tbs. ghee or clarified butter
½ fresh coconut, grated
1 Tbs. cumin seeds
1 Tbs. white poppy seeds
1 tsp. black peppercorns
1 tsp. turmeric
½ tsp. grated nutmeg
2 medium onions, chopped
½kg./1lb. potatoes, cubed

1 tsp. salt
2 cups thick coconut milk
2lb. lean lamb, cubed
5 Tbs. ghee or clarified butter
½ fresh coconut, grated
1 Tbs. cumin seeds
1 Tbs. white poppy seeds
1 tsp. black peppercorns
1 tsp. turmeric
½ tsp. grated nutmeg
2 medium onions, chopped
1lb. potatoes, cubed

Thayir Kari is a traditional dish made with lamb and yogurt.

Put the chillis, coriander leaves, garlic, ginger and salt into a blender and blend with 2 to 3 tablespoons of the coconut milk to a smooth purée. Transfer to a large bowl and stir in the meat cubes. Set aside at room temperature for 6 hours.

Melt 2 tablespoons of ghee or clarified butter in a frying-pan. Add the grated coconut and spices and fry for 5 minutes, stirring constantly. Remove from the heat and set the mixture aside to cool. Put into the blender with 125ml./4fl.oz. (½ cup) of the remaining coconut milk and blend to a smooth purée. Set aside.

Melt the remaining ghee in a large saucepan. Add the onions and fry, stirring occasionally, until they are brown. Add the coconut and spice purée and fry for 5 minutes, stirring constantly. Add the meat and chilli mixture and fry until the cubes are evenly browned. Pour in the remaining coconut milk and bring to the boil. Cover the pan, reduce the heat to low and simmer for 45 minutes.

Add the potatoes and simmer, uncovered, for a further 30 minutes, or until the meat and potatoes are cooked through and tender, and the sauce has thickened.

Transfer the shakooti to a warmed serving dish and serve at once.

Serves 4-6
Preparation and cooking time: 7¾ hours

Sag Gosht

(Spinach with Meat)

Metric/Imperial	American
50g./2oz. butter	4 Tbs. butter
1½ tsp. mustard seeds	1½ tsp. mustard seeds
2 garlic cloves, crushed	2 garlic cloves, crushed
1 Tbs. cardamom seeds	1 Tbs. cardamom seeds
1 Tbs. ground coriander	1 Tbs. ground coriander
4cm./1½in. piece of fresh root ginger, peeled and chopped	1½in. piece of fresh green ginger, peeled and chopped
1kg./2lb. lean lamb, cubed	2lb. lean lamb, cubed
1 medium onion, chopped	1 medium onion, chopped
3 green chillis, chopped	3 green chillis, chopped
1 tsp. sugar	1 tsp. sugar
1 tsp. turmeric	1 tsp. turmeric
1kg./2lb. spinach, washed and chopped	2lb. spinach, washed and chopped
1½ tsp. salt	1½ tsp. salt
½ tsp. black pepper	½ tsp. black pepper
3 Tbs. yogurt	3 Tbs. yogurt

Melt the butter in a flameproof casserole. Add the mustard seeds and cover. When they begin to spatter, stir in the garlic, cardamom, coriander and ginger. Fry for 1 minute, stirring constantly. Add the lamb cubes and fry until they are evenly browned. Add the onion, chillis and sugar and fry, stirring occasionally, until the onions are golden brown. Stir in the turmeric and spinach and cook for 3 minutes. Stir in the remaining ingredients. Cover the casserole, reduce the heat to low and simmer for 1 hour. Uncover and stir well to mix.

Preheat the oven to cool 150°C (Gas Mark 2, 300°F). Transfer the casserole to the oven and cook for 25 minutes, or until the lamb is cooked through and tender.

Serve at once, from the casserole.

Serves 4-6
Preparation and cooking time: 1¾ hours

Zeera Gosht

(Cumin Lamb)

Metric/Imperial	American
1 Tbs. cumin seeds	1 Tbs. cumin seeds
2½cm./1in. piece of fresh root ginger, peeled and chopped	1in. piece of fresh green ginger, peeled and chopped
2 garlic cloves	2 garlic cloves
2 tsp. cardamom seeds	2 tsp. cardamom seeds
2 cloves	2 cloves
10 blanched almonds	10 blanched almonds
2 tsp. sesame seeds	2 tsp. sesame seeds
1 tsp. cayenne pepper	1 tsp. cayenne pepper
1 tsp. salt	1 tsp. salt
1 tsp. soft brown sugar	1 tsp. soft brown sugar
175ml./6fl.oz. yogurt	¾ cup yogurt

40g./1½oz. butter	3 Tbs. butter
1 medium onion, chopped	1 medium onion, chopped
2 large green peppers, pith and seeds removed and chopped	2 large green peppers, pith and seeds removed and chopped
1kg./2lb. lean lamb, cubed	2lb. lean lamb, cubed
¼ tsp. ground saffron	¼ tsp. ground saffron

Put the cumin seeds, ginger, garlic, cardamom seeds, cloves, almonds, sesame seeds, cayenne, salt, sugar and 2 tablespoons of yogurt into a blender and blend to a smooth purée, adding more yogurt if necessary. Transfer to a small bowl.

Melt the butter in a large flameproof casserole. Add the onion and fry, stirring occasionally, until it is golden brown. Stir in the spice paste and fry for 5 minutes, stirring constantly. Add a spoonful or two of water if the mixture becomes too dry. Add the peppers and fry for 2 minutes. Add the lamb and fry for 10 minutes, turning frequently.

Meanwhile, beat the yogurt and saffron together, then pour into the meat mixture and mix well. Bring to the boil, cover and reduce the heat to very low. Simmer for 50 minutes.

Meanwhile, preheat the oven to cool 150°C (Gas Mark 2, 300°F). Transfer the casserole to the oven and cook the lamb for 25 minutes. Remove from the oven and serve at once.

Serves 4-6
Preparation and cooking time: 2 hours

Nargisi Koftas

(Meatballs Stuffed with Hard-boiled Eggs)

Metric/Imperial	American
575g./1¼lb. minced lamb	1¼lb. ground lamb
2½cm./1in. piece of fresh root ginger, peeled and chopped	1in. piece of fresh green ginger, peeled and chopped
½ tsp. hot chilli powder	½ tsp. hot chilli powder
1 tsp. ground cumin	1 tsp. ground cumin
1 Tbs. ground coriander	1 Tbs. ground coriander
1 onion, finely chopped	1 onion, finely chopped
2 garlic cloves, crushed	2 garlic cloves, crushed
40g./1½oz. gram or chick-pea flour	⅓ cup gram or chick-pea flour
1 tsp. salt	1 tsp. salt
½ tsp. black pepper	½ tsp. black pepper
1 egg	1 egg
8 hard-boiled eggs	8 hard-boiled eggs
vegetable oil for deep-frying	vegetable oil for deep-frying

Combine all the ingredients, except the hard-boiled eggs and oil, together until they are well blended. Divide the mixture into eight equal portions. Using damp hands, roll each portion into a ball, then flatten with the palm of your hands. Put a hard-boiled egg in the centre of the meat and bring the meat up and around it, to enclose it completely. Put the balls in a greased dish and chill in the refrigerator for 30 minutes.

Fill a large deep-frying pan one-third full with oil and heat until it is hot. Carefully lower the meatballs into the oil, a few at a time, and fry for 2 to 3 minutes, or until they are crisp and golden brown. Transfer to kitchen towels to drain.

Arrange the koftas on a warmed serving dish and serve hot.

Serves 4

Preparation and cooking time: 30 minutes

Turkari Molee

(Lamb and Coconut Curry)

Metric/Imperial	American
50g./2oz. butter	4 Tbs. butter
2 medium onions, sliced	2 medium onions, sliced
6 garlic cloves, crushed	6 garlic cloves, crushed
5cm./2in. piece of fresh root ginger, peeled and chopped	2in. piece of fresh green ginger, peeled and chopped
1½ tsp. turmeric	1½ tsp. turmeric
2 tsp. hot chilli powder	2 tsp. hot chilli powder
½ tsp. black pepper	½ tsp. black pepper
½ tsp. ground fenugreek	½ tsp. ground fenugreek
2 tsp. ground coriander	2 tsp. ground coriander
1 tsp. ground cumin	1 tsp. ground cumin
2 tsp. paprika	2 tsp. paprika
1kg./2lb. lean lamb, cubed	2lb lean lamb, cubed
600ml./1 pint coconut milk	2½ cups coconut milk
1½ tsp. salt	1½ tsp. salt
2 curry leaves (optional)	2 curry leaves (optional)

Melt the butter in a large saucepan. Add the onions and fry, stirring occasionally, until they are golden brown. Add the garlic, ginger and spices and fry for 5 minutes, stirring frequently. Add a spoonful or two of water if the mixture becomes too dry.

Add the lamb cubes and fry until they are evenly browned. Pour over the coconut milk, salt and curry leaves, if used, and bring to the boil. Cover the pan, reduce the heat to low and simmer for 1¼ hours, or until the lamb is cooked through and tender.

Transfer to a warmed serving dish and serve at once.

Serves 4-6

Preparation and cooking time: 1½ hours

Jal Farazi

(Curried Lamb and Potatoes)

This spicy lamb curry, Turkari Molee, should be served with rice and chutneys and an interesting accompaniment is Turkari Aloo, a hot vegetable dish made with potatoes.

Metric/Imperial	American
50ml./2fl.oz. vegetable oil	¼ cup vegetable oil
2 onions, sliced	2 onions, sliced
1 garlic clove, crushed	1 garlic clove, crushed
2½cm./1in. piece of fresh root ginger, peeled and chopped	1in. piece of fresh green ginger, peeled and chopped

Metric/Imperial	American
2 green chillis, finely chopped	2 green chillis, finely chopped
1 tsp. turmeric	1 tsp. turmeric
1 tsp. mustard seeds	1 tsp. mustard seeds
700g./1½lb. cooked lamb, cubed	1½lb. cooked lamb, cubed
½kg./1lb. potatoes, cooked and cubed	1lb. potatoes, cooked and cubed
1 tsp. salt	1 tsp. salt
juice of ½ lemon	juice of ½ lemon

Heat the oil in a large frying-pan. When it is hot, add the onions and garlic and fry, stirring occasionally, until the onions are soft. Add the ginger and chillis and fry for 2 minutes. Stir in the turmeric and mustard seeds and fry for 1 minute, stirring frequently.

Stir in the lamb, potatoes and salt and fry, stirring constantly, until they are well coated in the spices. Stir in the lemon juice and a spoonful or two of water if the mixture becomes too dry. Cook for 3 to 5 minutes, or until the mixture is quite dry and very hot.
Serves 4
Preparation and cooking time: 15 minutes

Biryani

(Spiced Rice with Lamb)

Metric/Imperial	American
125g./4oz. ghee or clarified butter	8 Tbs. ghee or clarified butter
2 garlic cloves, crushed	2 garlic cloves, crushed
2½cm./1in. piece of fresh root ginger, peeled and chopped	1in. piece of fresh green ginger, peeled and chopped
¼ tsp. cayenne pepper	¼ tsp. cayenne pepper
1½ tsp. cumin seeds	1½ tsp. cumin seeds
1kg./2lb. lean lamb, cubed	2lb. lean lamb, cubed
10cm./4in. cinnamon stick	4in. cinnamon stick
10 cloves	10 cloves
8 peppercorns	8 peppercorns
1 tsp. cardamom seeds	1 tsp. cardamon seeds
300ml./10fl.oz. yogurt	1¼ cups yogurt
2 tsp. salt	2 tsp. salt
450g./1lb. long-grain rice, soaked in cold water for 30 minutes and drained	2⅔ cups long-grain rice, soaked in cold water for 30 minutes and drained
½ tsp. saffron threads, soaked in 2 Tbs. boiling water	½ tsp. saffron threads, soaked in 2 Tbs. boiling water
2 onions, thinly sliced	2 onions, thinly sliced
40g./1½oz. slivered almonds	⅓ cup slivered almonds
40g./1½oz. pistachio nuts	⅓ cup pistachio nuts
50g./2oz. sultanans	⅓ cup seedless raisins

Melt half the ghee or clarified butter in a large saucepan. Add the garlic, ginger, cayenne and cumin seeds and fry for 3 minutes, stirring frequently. Add the lamb cubes and fry until they are deeply and evenly browned. Stir in the spices, yogurt and 1 teaspoon of salt. Add 150ml./5fl.oz. (⅔ cup) of water and bring to the boil, stirring occasionally. Cover the pan, reduce the heat to low and simmer for 1 hour, or until the lamb is cooked through and tender.

Bring 1¾l./3 pints (7½ cups) of water to the boil in a large saucepan. Add the remaining salt and the rice and boil briskly for 1½ minutes. Remove from the

heat, drain the rice thoroughly and set aside.

Preheat the oven to moderate 180°C (Gas Mark 4, 350°F).

Put 1 tablespoon of ghee or clarified butter into a large ovenproof casserole. Put one-third of the rice over the bottom and sprinkle one-third of the saffron mixture over it. Cover with a layer of one-third of the lamb. Continue making layers in this way until the ingredients are used up, ending with a layer of rice sprinkled with saffron. Pour all the liquid remaining in the pan containing the meat over the casserole mixture. Cover and put the dish into the oven. Cook for 20 to 30 minutes, or until the rice is cooked and the liquid is absorbed.

Melt the remaining ghee or clarified butter in a frying-pan. Add the onions and fry, stirring occasionally, until they are golden brown. Using a slotted spoon, transfer them to drain on kitchen towels. Add the remaining ingredients to the pan and fry for 3 minutes, or until the nuts are lightly browned. Set aside.

Remove the casserole from the oven and sprinkle the onions, nuts and sultanas (raisins) over the top before serving.

Serves 6
Preparation and cooking time: 2¼ hours

Biryani is a delicate mixture of lamb, spices, nuts and saffron rice and forms a complete meal in itself.

43

Raan is a very exotic, Indian dish made with leg of lamb marinated in spiced yogurt for 45 hours.

Raan

(Leg of Lamb Marinated in Spiced Yogurt)

Metric/Imperial	American
1 x 3kg./6lb. leg of lamb	1 x 6lb. leg of lamb
125g./4oz. fresh root ginger, peeled and chopped	4oz. fresh green ginger, peeled and chopped
12 large garlic cloves, crushed	12 large garlic cloves, crushed
thinly pared rind of 1 lemon	thinly pared rind of 1 lemon
5 Tbs. lemon juice	5 Tbs. lemon juice
2 tsp. cumin seeds	2 tsp. cumin seeds
2 Tbs. cardamom seeds	2 Tbs. cardamom seeds
8 cloves	8 cloves
1 tsp. turmeric	1 tsp. turmeric
1½ tsp. hot chilli powder	1½ tsp. hot chilli powder
1 Tbs. salt	1 Tbs. salt
150g./5oz. unblanched almonds	1 cup unblanched almonds
4 Tbs. soft brown sugar	4 Tbs. soft brown sugar
300ml./10fl.oz. yogurt	1¼ cups yogurt

½ tsp. saffron threads, soaked in
  2 Tbs. boiling water

½ tsp. saffron threads, soaked in
  2 Tbs. boiling water

Prick the lamb all over, then make several deep slits in the flesh. Put the lamb in a deep roasting pan.

Put the ginger, garlic, lemon rind and juice, spices and salt in a blender and blend to a smooth purée. Spread the purée all over the meat and set aside at room temperature for 1 hour.

Meanwhile, put the almonds, 2 tablespoons of sugar and half the yogurt into the blender and blend to a smooth purée. Transfer the purée to a bowl and stir in the remaining yogurt. Spread the mixture all over the lamb, on top of the spice purée. Cover the pan and put into the refrigerator for 45 hours.

Preheat the oven to hot 220°C (Gas Mark 7, 425°F). Remove the roasting pan from the refrigerator and allow the meat to warm to room temperature. Sprinkle over the remaining sugar.

Put the pan into the oven and roast, uncovered, for 20 minutes. Reduce the temperature to moderate 180°C (Gas Mark 4, 350°F) and roast for 1 hour. Reduce the temperature to warm 170°C (Gas Mark 3, 325°F), cover the pan and cook, basting occasionally, for 4 hours. Remove from the oven and very carefully transfer the meat to a large piece of foil. Cover completely and return to the oven.

Skim any scum from the surface of the cooking liquid and stir in the saffron mixture. Set the pan over moderately high heat and boil briskly for 15 to 20 minutes, or until the sauce has reduced by about half.

Remove the lamb from the oven and discard the foil. Arrange on a warmed serving dish, spoon over the sauce and serve.

Serves 8
Preparation and cooking time: 54 hours

Badami Gosht

(Lamb Cooked with Almonds)

Metric/Imperial	American
5 Tbs. vegetable oil	5 Tbs. vegetable oil
2 cinnamon sticks	2 cinnamon sticks
6 cloves	6 cloves
1 Tbs. cardamom seeds	1 Tbs. cardamom seeds
1 large onion, chopped	1 large onion, chopped
2 garlic cloves, crushed	2 garlic cloves, crushed
4cm./1½in. piece of fresh root ginger, peeled and chopped	1½in. piece of fresh green ginger, peeled and chopped
700g./1½lb. lean lamb, cubed	1½lb. lean lamb, cubed
300ml./10fl.oz. yogurt	1¼ cups yogurt
1 tsp. saffron threads, soaked in 2 Tbs. boiling water	1 tsp. saffron threads, soaked in 2 Tbs. boiling water
½ tsp. hot chilli powder	½ tsp. hot chilli powder
75g./3oz. ground almonds	½ cup ground almonds
1 tsp. salt	1 tsp. salt
350ml./12fl.oz. coconut milk	1½ cups coconut milk
2 dried red chillis	2 dried red chillis

Heat the oil in a saucepan. When it is hot, add the cinnamon, cloves and cardamom and fry for 1 minute. Add the onion and fry, stirring occasionally, until it is soft. Add the garlic and ginger and fry for 3 minutes, stirring frequently. Add the lamb cubes and fry until they are evenly browned.

Beat the yogurt, saffron mixture and chilli powder together, then stir mixture into the lamb cubes. Cook for 1 minute.

Beat the almonds with enough water to form a thick paste, then stir the paste into the lamb cubes, with the salt. Simmer for 15 minutes. Stir in the coconut milk and chillis and reduce the heat to low. Simmer for 1 hour, or until the lamb is cooked through and tender. Uncover the pan for the last 10 minutes of cooking.

Transfer to a warmed serving dish and serve at once.

Serves 4
Preparation and cooking time: 1½ hours

Samosas

(Stuffed Savoury Pastries)

Metric/Imperial	American
PASTRY	PASTRY
225g./8oz. flour	2 cups flour
½ tsp. salt	½ tsp. salt
25g./1oz. butter	2 Tbs. butter

Samosas, crisp pastry balls with a spicy meat or vegetable filling, are delicious either as a snack or as an accompaniment to a meal.

50-75ml./2-3fl.oz. water

FILLING

25g./1oz. butter

1 small onion, chopped

2 garlic cloves, crushed

2 green chillis, chopped

2½cm./1in. piece of fresh root ginger, peeled and chopped

½ tsp. turmeric

½ tsp. hot chilli powder

350g./12oz. minced lamb

1 tsp. salt

2 tsp. garam masala

juice of ½ lemon

vegetable oil for deep-frying

¼-⅓ cup water

FILLING

2 Tbs. butter

1 small onion, chopped

2 garlic cloves, crushed

2 green chillis, chopped

1in. piece of fresh green ginger, peeled and chopped

½ tsp. turmeric

½ tsp. hot chilli powder

12oz. ground lamb

1 tsp. salt

2 tsp. garam masala

juice of ½ lemon

vegetable oil for deep-frying

First make the pastry. Sift the flour and salt into a bowl. Add the butter and rub it into the flour until the mixture resembles fine breadcrumbs. Pour in 50ml./ 2fl.oz. (¼ cup) of water and mix to a smooth dough. Add a little more water if the dough is too dry. Pat into a ball and turn out on to a lightly floured surface. Knead for 10 minutes, or until the dough is smooth and elastic. Return to the bowl, cover and set aside.

Melt the butter in a frying-pan. Add the onion, garlic, chillis and ginger and fry, stirring occasionally, until the onions are golden brown. Stir in the spices, then add the meat and salt and fry until the meat loses its pinkness. Stir in the garam masala and lemon juice and cook for 5 minutes, stirring occasionally. Remove from the heat and set aside to cool.

Divide the dough into 15 equal portions. Roll each portion into a ball, flatten and roll out to a circle about 10cm./4in. in diameter. Cut each circle in half. Dampen the cut edges of the semi-circles and shape into cones. Fill the cones with a little of the filling, dampen the top and bottom edges and pinch together to seal.

Fill a deep-frying pan one-third full with oil and heat until it is hot. Carefully lower the samosas into the oil, a few at a time, and fry for 2 to 3 minutes, or until they are golden brown and crisp. Drain on kitchen towels.

Pile into a warmed serving dish and serve at once.

Makes 30 Samosas
Preparation and cooking time: 45 minutes

Kamargaah

(Lamb Chops in Batter)

Metric/Imperial	American
8 lamb chops or cutlets	8 lamb chops or cutlets
350ml./12fl.oz. milk	1½ cups water
175ml./6fl.oz. water	¾ cup water
½ tsp. salt	½ tsp. salt
2 tsp. crushed cardamom seeds	2 tsp. crushed cardamom seeds
6 whole cloves	6 whole cloves
1 tsp. crushed black peppercorns	1 tsp. crushed black peppercorns
125ml./4fl.oz. vegetable oil	½ cup vegetable oil
BATTER	BATTER
50g./2oz. chick-pea flour	½ cup chick-pea flour
½ tsp. hot chilli powder	½ tsp. hot chilli powder
1 tsp. ground coriander	1 tsp. ground coriander
1 tsp. garam masala	1 tsp. garam masala
1 Tbs. melted ghee or clarified butter	1 Tbs. melted ghee or clarified butter
2 Tbs. yogurt	2 Tbs. yogurt
125ml./4fl.oz. water	½ cup water

First make the batter. Combine the chick-pea flour, chilli powder, coriander and garam masala in a medium bowl. Gradually stir in the melted ghee, yogurt and water until the mixture forms a smooth, fairly thick batter. Set aside at room temperature for 20 minutes.

Meanwhile, put the meat into a large saucepan and add all the remaining ingredients except the oil. Bring to the boil, reduce the heat to low and simmer, uncovered, for 30 to 40 minutes, or until the chops are cooked through and tender and the liquid evaporates. Remove from the heat and remove the chops from the pan.

Heat the oil in a large frying-pan. When it is very hot, dip the chops in the batter to coat them thoroughly, then arrange them in the pan. Fry for 5 minutes on each side, or until they are golden brown. Remove them from the pan and drain on kitchen towels.

Serve at once.

Serves 4-8
Preparation and cooking time: 1½ hours

Dry Beef Curry

Metric/Imperial	American
kg./2lb. braising steak, cut into cubes	2lb. chunk steak, cut into cubes
0g./2oz. seasoned flour	½ cup seasoned flour
Tbs. dried red chillis, crumbled	1 Tbs. dried red chillis, crumbled
Tbs. fennel seeds	1 Tbs. fennel seeds
whole bulb of garlic, crushed	1 whole bulb of garlic, crushed
cm./1½in. piece of fresh root ginger, peeled and chopped	1½in. piece of fresh green ginger, peeled and chopped
Tbs. ground coriander	2 Tbs. ground coriander
tsp. ground cumin	1 tsp. ground cumin
Tbs. ground cloves	1 Tbs. ground cloves
Tbs. ground cinnamon	1 Tbs. ground cinnamon
tsp. ground fenugreek	1 tsp. ground fenugreek
Tbs. white wine vinegar	3 Tbs. white wine vinegar
0g./2oz. ghee or clarified butter	4 Tbs. ghee or clarified butter
onions, chopped	2 onions, chopped
00ml./1 pint beef stock	2½ cups beef stock

Roll the beef cubes in the seasoned flour, shaking off any excess. Set aside.

Combine the chillis, fennel seeds, garlic and ginger and put them into a blender. Blend to a smooth purée. Transfer the purée to a small bowl and stir in the coriander, cumin, cloves, cinnamon and fenugreek until they are well blended. Stir in the vinegar until the mixture forms a smooth paste.

Melt the ghee in a large saucepan. Add the spice paste and cook, stirring constantly, for 2 minutes. Reduce the heat to low and cook for a further 2 minutes, stirring constantly. Add the onions to the pan and cook, stirring occasionally, until they are soft.

Add the meat and cook until it is evenly browned. Pour over the beef stock and bring to the boil. Reduce the heat to low, cover the saucepan and simmer the mixture for 2 to 2½ hours, or until the beef is tender.

Transfer the mixture to a warmed serving bowl and serve at once.

Serves 4-6
Preparation and cooking time: 3 hours

Harak Muss

(Sri Lankan Beef Curry)

Metric/Imperial	American
50g./2oz. ghee or clarified butter	4 Tbs. ghee or clarified butter
2 medium onions, chopped	2 medium onions, chopped
2 garlic cloves, crushed	2 garlic cloves, crushed
4cm./1½in. piece of fresh root ginger, peeled and chopped	1½in. piece of fresh green ginger, peeled and chopped
1 tsp. chopped lemon grass or grated lemon rind	1 tsp. chopped lemon grass or grated lemon rind
1 Tbs. lemon juice	1 Tbs. lemon juice
1 tsp. turmeric	1 tsp. turmeric
2 red chillis, chopped	2 red chillis, chopped
1kg./2lb. braising steak, cut into cubes	2lb. chuck steak, cut into cubes

200g./7oz. tin tomatoes	7oz. can tomatoes
250ml./8fl.oz. thick coconut milk	1 cup thick coconut milk
MASALA	MASALA
2 tsp. coriander seeds	2 tsp. coriander seeds
1 tsp. cumin seeds	1 tsp. cumin seeds
½ tsp. fennel seeds	½ tsp. fennel seeds
2.5cm./1in. cinnamon stick	1in. cinnamon stick
5 whole cloves	5 whole cloves
¼ tsp. cardamom seeds	¼ tsp. cardamom seeds

First make the masala. Arrange the spices, except the chillis, separately on a large baking sheet and dry roast them for 5 minutes in a moderate preheated oven. Remove from the oven and transfer them to a blender. Alternatively, dry roast the spices separately in a frying-pan for 3 minutes over gentle heat. Remove from the pan and put into a blender. Blend the mixture to a powder and set aside.

Melt the ghee in a large saucepan. Add the onions, garlic and ginger and fry, stirring occasionally, until the onions are soft. Stir in the masala mixture, the lemon grass or rind, lemon juice, turmeric and chopped chillis and continue frying for 5 minutes, stirring frequently. Add a spoonful or two of water if the mixture becomes too dry. Add the beef cubes and fry until they are evenly browned and coated with the spice mixture.

Stir in the tomatoes and can juice and the coconut milk and bring to the boil. Reduce the heat to low, cover the pan and simmer the mixture for 2 to 2½ hours, or until the beef is cooked and tender.

Transfer the mixture to a warmed serving dish and serve at once.
Serves 6
Preparation and cooking time: 3¼ hours

Gosht Aur Aloo

(Beef and Potato Curry)

Metric/Imperial	American
50g./2oz. ghee or clarified butter	4 Tbs. ghee or clarified butter
2 onions, chopped	2 onions, chopped
1 garlic clove, crushed	1 garlic clove, crushed
4cm./1½in. piece of fresh root ginger, peeled and chopped	1½in. piece of fresh green ginger, peeled and chopped
2 green chillis, chopped	2 green chillis, chopped
1 tsp. turmeric	1 tsp. turmeric
1 Tbs. ground coriander	1 Tbs. ground coriander
¼ tsp. hot chilli powder	¼ tsp. hot chilli powder
1 tsp. ground cumin	1 tsp. ground cumin
2 Tbs. cardamom seeds, crushed	2 Tbs. cardamom seeds, crushed
½ tsp. ground cloves	½ tsp. ground cloves
1kg./2lb. stewing steak, cubed	2lb. chuck steak, cubed
450ml./15fl.oz. water	2 cups water
1 tsp. salt	1 tsp. salt
2 bay leaves	2 bay leaves
½kg. 1lb. potatoes, scrubbed	1lb. potatoes, scrubbed

Melt the ghee or clarified butter in a large saucepan. Add the onions and garlic and fry, stirring occasionally, until the onions are golden brown. Add the ginger and chillis and fry for 4 minutes, stirring frequently. Stir in the spices and fry for 6 minutes, stirring frequently. Add a spoonful or two of water if the mixture becomes too dry.

Stir in the meat cubes and fry until they are evenly browned. Stir in the water, salt and bay leaves and bring to the boil. Cover the pan, reduce the heat to low and simmer the mixture for 1¼ hours. Add the potatoes and bring to the boil again. Re-cover and simmer for a further 45 minutes, or until the meat is cooked through.

Transfer to a warmed serving dish and serve at once.

Serves 4-6

Preparation and cooking time: 2½ hours

Seekh Kabab

(Beef Kebabs)

Metric/Imperial	American
700g./1½lb. minced beef	1½lb. ground beef
50g./2oz. fresh breadcrumbs	1 cup fresh breadcrumbs
2½cm./1in. piece of fresh root ginger, peeled and chopped	1in. piece of fresh green ginger, peeled and chopped
1 green chilli, chopped	1 green chilli, chopped
2 garlic cloves, crushed	2 garlic cloves, crushed
1 tsp. ground cumin	1 tsp. ground cumin
½ tsp. hot chilli powder	½ tsp. hot chilli powder
½ tsp. salt	½ tsp. salt
1 tsp. grated lemon rind	1 tsp. grated lemon rind
1 tsp. lemon juice	1 tsp. lemon juice

Combine all the ingredients in a large bowl and knead to mix thoroughly.

Divide the meat mixture into 16 portions. With damp hands, press eight portions on to well-greased wooden skewers, into pencil shapes, gently pressing the meat mixture until the kebabs measure about 10cm./4in. in length.

Preheat the oven to cool 150°C (Gas Mark 2, 300°F) and then preheat the grill (broiler) to high.

Arrange the eight skewers beneath the heat and grill (broil) turning once, for 5 to 8 minutes, or until the kebabs are cooked through. Slide the kebabs off the

skewers and put into an ovenproof dish. Cover and put into the oven while you cook the remaining kebabs in the same way.
Serve at once.
Serves 4
Preparation and cooking time: 20 minutes

Kofta-Kabab Khatai

(Meatballs in Yogurt)

Metric/Imperial	American
1kg./2lb. minced beef	2lb. ground beef
4cm./1½in. piece of fresh root ginger, peeled and chopped	1½in. piece of fresh green ginger, peeled and chopped
2 garlic cloves, crushed	2 garlic cloves, crushed
125g./4oz. gram or chick-pea flour	1 cup gram or chick-pea flour
1¼ tsp. salt	1¼ tsp. salt
½ tsp. hot chilli powder	½ tsp. hot chilli powder
1 egg	1 egg
50g./2oz. sultanas	⅓ cup seedless raisins
juice of ½ lemon	juice of ½ lemon
3 Tbs. water	3 Tbs. water
75ml./3fl.oz. vegetable oil	⅓ cup vegetable oil
SAUCE	SAUCE
50g./2oz. butter	4 Tbs. butter
2 medium onions, chopped	2 medium onions, chopped
2½cm./1in. piece of fresh root ginger, peeled and chopped	1in. piece of fresh green ginger, peeled and chopped
2 garlic cloves, crushed	2 garlic cloves, crushed
1 Tbs. ground coriander	1 Tbs. ground coriander
1 tsp. ground cumin	1 tsp. ground cumin
½ tsp. hot chilli powder	½ tsp. hot chilli powder
600ml./1 pint yogurt	2½ cups yogurt
1 tsp. salt	1 tsp. salt
2 Tbs. chopped coriander leaves	2 Tbs. chopped coriander leaves

Combine the meat, ginger, garlic, 50g./2oz. (½ cup) of flour, 1 teaspoon of salt, the chilli powder and egg in a bowl. Knead until the ingredients are blended. Divide the mixture into about 34 portions. Roll each portion into a small ball, flatten and put 4 to 5 sultanas (raisins) in the centre. Shape the mixture around the sultanas or raisins to enclose them completely. Roll lightly to make them round and set aside.

Sift the remaining flour and salt into a saucer. Mix into a thick batter with the lemon juice and as much of the water as is necessary. Coat the meatballs in a little of the batter.

Heat the oil in a large frying-pan. When it is hot, add the meatballs and fry until they are golden brown. (Fry in several batches if necessary).

To make the sauce, melt the butter in a large saucepan. Add the onions, ginger and garlic and fry, stirring occasionally, until the onions are golden brown. Stir in the spices and fry for 3 minutes, stirring frequently. Stir in the yogurt and salt and bring to the boil. Gently stir in the meatballs, coating them thoroughly in the sauce. Cover the pan, reduce the heat to low and simmer for 15 minutes.

Transfer the mixture to a warmed serving dish and sprinkle over the coriander leaves before serving.
Serves 4-6
Preparation and cooking time: 1 hour

An alternative way of cooking meatballs is Kofta-kabab Khatai which are beef and raisin meatballs cooked in an aromatic yogurt sauce.

Pork Vindaloo

(Pork Vinegar Curry)

Metric/Imperial	American
5cm./2in. piece of fresh root ginger, peeled and chopped	2in. piece of fresh green ginger, peeled and chopped
4 garlic cloves, chopped	4 garlic cloves, chopped
1½ tsp. hot chilli powder	1½ tsp. hot chilli powder
2 tsp. turmeric	2 tsp. turmeric
1 tsp. salt	1 tsp. salt
2 tsp. cardamom seeds	2 tsp. cardamom seeds
6 cloves	6 cloves
6 peppercorns	6 peppercorns
1 cinnamon stick	1 cinnamon stick
2 Tbs. coriander seeds	2 Tbs. coriander seeds
1 Tbs. cumin seeds	1 Tbs. cumin seeds
150ml./5fl.oz. wine vinegar	⅔ cup wine vinegar
1kg./2lb. pork fillet, cubed	2lb. pork tenderloin, cubed
4 curry or bay leaves	4 curry or bay leaves
3 Tbs. vegetable oil	3 Tbs. vegetable oil
1 tsp. mustard seeds	1 tsp. mustard seeds
150ml./5fl.oz. water	⅔ cup water

Put the spices and vinegar into a blender and blend to a smooth purée, adding more liquid if necessary to form a liquid paste. Put the pork cubes into a large bowl and stir in the spice paste. Cover and set aside to marinate at room temperature for 1 hour. Lay the curry or bay leaves on top, re-cover and chill in the refrigerator for 24 hours, turning and basting the meat from time to time. Two hours before cooking time, remove the bowl from the refrigerator and set aside at room temperature.

Heat the oil in a large saucepan. Add the mustard seeds and cover the pan. When the seeds begin to spatter, add the pork, marinade and the water and bring to the boil. Cover the pan, reduce the heat to low and simmer for 40 minutes. Uncover the pan and simmer for a further 30 minutes, or until the pork is cooked through and tender and the sauce is neither too thick nor too thin.

Transfer the vindaloo to a warmed serving dish and serve at once.

Serves 4-6
Preparation and cooking time: 26½ hours

Pork Korma

(Braised Sliced Pork)

Metric/Imperial	American
50g./2oz. butter	4 Tbs. butter
4cm./1½oz. piece of fresh root ginger, peeled and chopped	1½in. piece of fresh green ginger, peeled and chopped
3 garlic cloves, crushed	3 garlic cloves, crushed
2 medium onions, chopped	2 medium onions, chopped
½ tsp. hot chilli powder	½ tsp. hot chilli powder
2 Tbs. ground coriander	2 Tbs. ground coriander
1kg./2lb. pork fillet, cubed	2lb. pork tenderloin, cubed
1 tsp. salt	1 tsp. salt
300ml./10fl.oz. yogurt	1¼ cups yogurt
125g./4oz. ground almonds	⅔ cup ground almonds
300ml./10fl.oz. double cream	1¼ cups heavy cream
½ tsp. ground cinnamon	½ tsp. ground cinnamon
¼ tsp. ground mace	¼ tsp. ground mace
½ tsp. ground cardamom	½ tsp. ground cardamom
¼ tsp. saffron threads, soaked in 2 Tbs. boiling water	¼ tsp. saffron threads, soaked in 2 Tbs. boiling water
GARNISH	GARNISH
2 medium onions, thinly sliced into rings and fried until crisp	2 medium onions, thinly sliced into rings and fried until crisp

Melt the butter in a large flameproof casserole. Add the ginger, garlic and onions and fry, stirring occasionally, until the onions are golden brown. Stir in the chilli powder and coriander and fry for 1 minute. Add the pork cubes and fry until they are evenly browned. Increase the heat to high and cook for a further 8 to 10 minutes, stirring constantly, or until all the cooking juices have evaporated. Reduce the heat to moderate.

Stir in salt and 50ml./2fl.oz. (¼ cup) of the yogurt, then stir in 50ml./2fl.oz. (¼ cup) more until it evaporates. Continue adding the yogurt in this way until all the yogurt is used up and there is no liquid in the pan. Remove from the heat and stir in the ground almonds and cream. Stir in the cinnamon, mace and cardamom and bring to the boil. Cover the pan, reduce the heat to low and simmer for 35 minutes, stirring occasionally. Stir in the saffron mixture.

Meanwhile, preheat the oven to moderate 180°C (Gas Mark 4, 350°F).

Transfer the casserole to the oven and cook for 15 to 20 minutes, or until the pork is cooked through and tender. Remove from the oven, garnish with the fried onions before serving.

Serves 4-6
Preparation and cooking time: $1\frac{3}{4}$ hours

Liver Dopeedzah

Metric/Imperial	American
10 cardamom pods	10 cardamom pods
2.5cm./1in. piece of fresh root ginger, peeled and chopped	1in. piece of fresh green ginger, peeled and chopped
$\frac{1}{4}$ tsp. cayenne pepper	$\frac{1}{4}$ tsp. cayenne pepper
2 Tbs. grated onion	2 Tbs. grated onion
4 garlic cloves, crushed	4 garlic cloves, crushed
200ml./7fl.oz. yogurt	1 cup yogurt
150g./5oz. ghee or clarified butter	10 Tbs. ghee or clarified butter
2kg./4lb. onions, half sliced and half minced	4lb. onions, half sliced and half minced
700g./1$\frac{1}{2}$lb. ox or lambs' liver, cut into strips $\frac{1}{2}$cm./$\frac{1}{4}$in. thick and 5cm./2in. long	1$\frac{1}{2}$lb. ox or lambs' liver, cut into strips $\frac{1}{4}$in. thick and 2in. long
2 Tbs. ground coriander	2 Tbs. ground coriander
$\frac{1}{4}$ tsp. salt	$\frac{1}{4}$ tsp. salt
150ml./5fl.oz. water	$\frac{2}{3}$ cup water
$\frac{1}{4}$ tsp. black pepper	$\frac{1}{4}$ tsp. black pepper
$\frac{1}{4}$ tsp. ground saffron	$\frac{1}{4}$ tsp. ground saffron
$\frac{1}{2}$ tsp. grated nutmeg	$\frac{1}{2}$ tsp. grated nutmeg

Split half the cardamom pods and put them in a mortar. Add the ginger, cayenne, grated onion and garlic and pound the mixture with a pestle. Add 1 teaspoon of yogurt and continue to pound until the mixture forms a smooth paste. Rub the paste all over the liver strips and set aside at room temperature for 2 hours.

Melt one-third of the ghee in a heavy-based saucepan. Add the minced onions and fry, stirring occasionally, until they are golden. Using a slotted spoon, transfer the onions to a pestle or to a chopping board. Pound into a paste with a pestle or the end of a rolling pin. Alternatively, they can be puréed in a blender. Set aside.

Add half the remaining ghee to the saucepan. When it has melted, add the liver strips and fry for 5 to 8 minutes, or until they are evenly browned.

Split the remaining cardamom pods and grind the seeds. Stir the ground seeds, the coriander and salt into the pan and cook for 3 minutes, stirring frequently.

Add the remaining ghee, then the sliced onions. Cook, stirring occasionally, until the onions are soft. Stir in the yogurt, about 2 tablespoons at a time and making each addition when the previous amount has been amalgamated. Add the water, stirring constantly until it forms a sauce. Reduce the heat to low, cover and simmer the mixture for 20 minutes, or until the sauce has almost disappeared.

Stir in the onion purée, black pepper, saffron and nutmeg and continue to simmer for a further 10 minutes.

Transfer the mixture to a warmed serving dish and serve at once.

Serves 4
Preparation and cooking time: $3\frac{1}{2}$ hours

(See over) Served with raita and naan, Pork Korma is a hot, spicy dish made with yogurt and cream.

Spiced Liver

Metric/Imperial	American
700g./1½lb. lamb's liver, thinly sliced	1½lb. lamb's liver, thinly sliced
5cm./2in. piece of fresh root ginger, peeled and chopped	2in. piece of fresh green ginger, peeled and chopped
4 garlic cloves, crushed	4 garlic cloves, crushed
1 tsp. salt	1 tsp. salt
1 tsp. hot chilli powder	1 tsp. hot chilli powder
½ tsp. black pepper	½ tsp. black pepper
juice of 1 lemon	juice of 1 lemon
75g./3oz. ghee or clarified butter	6 Tbs. ghee or clarified butter

Cut each liver slice in half lengthways and set aside.

Combine the ginger, garlic, salt, chilli powder, pepper and lemon juice together in a large bowl and add the liver slices. Turn and toss them in the mixture until they are thoroughly coated. Cover and set aside to marinate at room temperature for 1 hour.

Melt the ghee or clarified butter in a large frying-pan. Add the liver slices, a few at a time, and fry for 4 to 6 minutes, or until they are cooked through and evenly browned. Transfer to a warmed serving dish and serve at once.
Serves 4-6
Preparation and cooking time: 1½ hours

Gurda Korma

(Curried Kidneys)

Metric/Imperial	American
25g./1oz. butter	2 Tbs. butter
1 Tbs. vegetable oil	1 Tbs. vegetable oil
1 garlic clove, crushed	1 garlic clove, crushed
1cm./½in. piece of fresh root ginger, peeled and chopped	½in. piece of fresh green ginger, peeled and chopped
2 small onions, chopped	2 small onions, chopped
¼ tsp. hot chilli powder	¼ tsp. hot chilli powder
¼ tsp. turmeric	¼ tsp. turmeric
1 tsp. ground coriander	1 tsp. ground coriander
¼ tsp. ground cumin	¼ tsp. ground cumin
¼ tsp. salt	¼ tsp. salt
½ tsp. black pepper	½ tsp. black pepper
8 lambs' kidneys, cored and halved	8 lambs' kidneys, cored and halved
1 small green pepper, pith and seeds removed and sliced	1 small green pepper, pith and seeds removed and sliced

Melt the butter and oil in a frying-pan. Add the garlic and ginger and fry for 30 seconds, stirring constantly. Add the onions and fry, stirring occasionally, until they are golden brown. Stir in the spices and cook for 1 minute. Add the salt, pepper and kidneys and stir to coat them with the spices. Cook for 15 minutes, stirring occasionally, or until the kidneys are cooked and tender.

Transfer the mixture to a warmed serving dish and garnish with the pepper slices before serving.
Serves 4
Preparation and cooking time: 30 minutes

Gurda Korma, complemented by home-made chutneys, is an appetizing meal of curried kidneys and green peppers.

POULTRY & GAME

Yogurt Chicken

Metric/Imperial	American
1 x 2kg./4lb. chicken, skinned	1 x 4lb. chicken, skinned
1 tsp. salt	1 tsp. salt
juice of ½ lemon	juice of ½ lemon
2 green chillis, finely chopped	2 green chillis, finely chopped
250ml./8fl.oz. yogurt	1 cup yogurt
½ bunch coriander leaves, finely chopped	½ bunch coriander leaves, finely chopped
5cm./2in. piece of fresh root ginger, peeled and chopped	2in. piece of fresh green ginger, peeled and chopped
4 garlic cloves, crushed	4 garlic cloves, crushed
50g./2oz. butter, melted	4 Tbs. butter, melted

Prick the chicken all over, then rub with the salt, lemon juice and chillis. Put into a large bowl and set aside for 30 minutes.

Combine the yogurt, coriander leaves, ginger and garlic, then rub the mixture all over the chicken. Cover and set aside for 8 hours.

Preheat the oven to fairly hot 200°C (Gas Mark 6, 400°F).

Pour half the butter into a roasting pan. Put the chicken and marinade into the pan and put into the oven. Roast for 20 minutes. Reduce the heat to moderate 180°C (Gas Mark 4, 350°F) and roast the chicken for a further 30 minutes, or until it is cooked through and tender, basting frequently with the remaining butter. Remove from the oven.

Transfer the chicken to a warmed serving dish. Put the pan over moderate heat and bring the juices to the boil, stirring constantly. Boil for about 5 minutes, or until they have thickened.

Pour the sauce over the chicken and serve at once.

Serves 4
Preparation and cooking time: 9¾ hours

Murg Tikka

(Chicken Kebabs)

Metric/Imperial	American
150ml./5fl.oz. yogurt	⅔ cup yogurt
4 garlic cloves, crushed	4 garlic cloves, crushed
4cm./1½in. piece of fresh root ginger, peeled and chopped	1½in. piece of fresh green ginger, peeled and chopped
1 small onion, grated	1 small onion, grated
1½ tsp. hot chilli powder	1½ tsp. hot chilli powder
1 Tbs. ground coriander	1 Tbs. ground coriander
1 tsp. salt	1 tsp. salt
3 chicken breasts, skinned and boned	3 chicken breasts, skinned and boned
GARNISH	GARNISH
1 large onion, sliced into rings	1 large onion, sliced into rings

Yogurt Chicken is roasted in yogurt and spices which combine to make a delightful North Indian meal.

61

2 large tomatoes, thinly sliced
2 Tbs. chopped coriander leaves

2 large tomatoes, thinly sliced
2 Tbs. chopped coriander leaves

Combine the yogurt, garlic, ginger, onion, chilli powder, coriander and salt. Cut the chicken meat into 2½cm./1in. cubes and stir into the marinade. Cover and chill in the refrigerator for at least 6 hours, or overnight, basting occasionally.

Preheat the grill (broiler) to high.

Thread the chicken cubes on to skewers and arrange them on the rack of the grill (broiler). Grill (broil) for 5 to 6 minutes, turning occasionally, or until they are cooked through. Remove from the heat.

Slide the chicken cubes from the skewers on to a warmed serving dish and garnish with the onion rings, tomato slices and chopped coriander before serving.
Serves 4
Preparation and cooking time: 7 hours

Chicken Vindaloo

Metric/Imperial	American
1 x 2½kg./5lb. chicken, skinned and cut into serving pieces	1 x 5lb. chicken, skinned and cut into serving pieces
1½ tsp. salt	1½ tsp. salt
½ tsp. cayenne pepper	½ tsp. cayenne pepper
2 tsp. lemon juice	2 tsp. lemon juice
2 dried red chillis	2 dried red chillis
4 garlic cloves	4 garlic cloves
4cm./1½in. piece of fresh root ginger, peeled and chopped	1½in. piece of fresh green ginger, peeled and chopped
1 tsp. cumin seeds	1 tsp. cumin seeds
2 tsp. coriander seeds	2 tsp. coriander seeds
1 tsp. black peppercorns	1 tsp. black peppercorns
1 cinnamon stick	1 cinnamon stick
4 cloves	4 cloves
2 Tbs. malt vinegar	2 Tbs. malt vinegar
3 Tbs. vegetable oil	3 Tbs. vegetable oil
2 medium onions, chopped	2 medium onions, chopped
1 tsp. turmeric	1 tsp. turmeric
300ml./10fl.oz. chicken stock	1¼ cups chicken stock

Rub the chicken pieces all over with half the salt, the cayenne and lemon juice. Set aside for 30 minutes.

Meanwhile put the spices and vinegar into a blender and blend to a purée, adding more vinegar if necessary. Transfer to a bowl.

Heat the oil in a saucepan. When it is hot, add the onions and fry, stirring occasionally, until they are golden brown. Stir in the turmeric and spice purée and fry for 5 minutes, stirring frequently. Add a spoonful or two of water if the mixture becomes too dry. Add the chicken pieces and fry until they are evenly browned. Pour in the stock and remaining salt and bring to the boil. Cover the pan, reduce the heat to low and simmer for 45 minutes, or until the chicken is cooked through and tender.

Spoon the vindaloo into a warmed serving dish and serve at once.
Serves 6
Preparation and cooking time: 1¾ hours

Derived from a traditional Indian dish, Chicken Vindaloo is a hot, colourful curry from Bombay.

Kashmiri Chicken

Metric/Imperial	American
1 medium onion, chopped	1 medium onion, chopped
5cm./2in. piece of fresh root ginger, peeled and chopped	2in. piece of fresh green ginger, peeled and chopped
2 garlic cloves, crushed	2 garlic cloves, crushed
1 tsp. coriander seeds	1 tsp. coriander seeds
1½ tsp. anchovy essence	1½ tsp. anchovy essence
250g./9oz. ground almonds·	1½ cups ground almonds
3 Tbs. vegetable oil	3 Tbs. vegetable oil
4 chicken pieces	4 chicken pieces
300ml./10fl.oz. chicken stock	1¼ cups chicken stock
300ml./10fl.oz. thick coconut milk	1¼ cups thick coconut milk
2 tsp. soft brown sugar	2 tsp. soft brown sugar
GARNISH	GARNISH
2 Tbs. finely chopped coriander leaves	2 Tbs. finely chopped coriander leaves
4 lemon wedges	4 lemon wedges

Combine the onion, ginger, garlic, coriander seeds and anchovy essence and put them into a blender. Blend to a smooth purée. Transfer the purée to a small bowl and stir in the ground almonds until the mixture is well blended.

Heat the oil in a saucepan. When it is hot, add the spice paste and fry, stirring constantly, for 5 minutes. Add a spoonful or two of water if the mixture becomes too dry.

Add the chicken pieces to the pan and turn until they are well coated with the spice mixture. Reduce the heat to moderately low and cook the chicken for 15 minutes, turning occasionally.

Pour over the chicken stock and bring to the boil, stirring constantly. Reduce the heat to low, cover the pan and simmer the mixture for 20 minutes. Stir in the coconut milk and brown sugar and continue to simmer the mixture for a further 20 minutes, or until the chicken is cooked through and tender.

Transfer the mixture to a warmed serving bowl and garnish with the coriander leaves and lemon wedges before serving.

Serves 4
Preparation and cooking time: 1¼ hours

63

Tandoori Murg is a very popular chicken dish, traditionally served with mixed salad.

Tandoori Murg

(Marinated Spiced Chicken)

Metric/Imperial	American
1 x 1½kg./3lb. chicken, skinned	1 x 3lb. chicken, skinned
1 tsp. hot chilli powder	1 tsp. hot chilli powder
1 tsp. salt	1 tsp. salt
½ tsp. black pepper	½ tsp. black pepper
2 Tbs. lemon juice	2 Tbs. lemon juice
50g./2oz. butter, melted	4 Tbs. butter, melted
MARINADE	MARINADE
3 Tbs. yogurt	3 Tbs. yogurt
4 garlic cloves	4 garlic cloves
1 Tbs. raisins	1 Tbs. raisins
5cm./2in. piece of fresh root ginger, peeled and chopped	2in. piece of fresh green ginger, peeled and chopped
1 tsp. cumin seeds	1 tsp. cumin seeds
1 Tbs. coriander seeds	1 Tbs. coriander seeds
2 dried red chillis	2 dried red chillis
½ tsp. red food colouring	½ tsp. red food coloring

Make gashes in the thighs and on each side of the breast of the chicken. Mix the chilli powder, salt, pepper and lemon juice together, then rub the mixture all over the chicken, especially into the gashes. Set aside for 20 minutes.

Meanwhile, prepare the marinade. Put all the ingredients, except the food colouring, into the blender and blend to a smooth purée. Transfer to a bowl and mix in the food colouring. Put the chicken into a large bowl, then spread the mixture all over the chicken, rubbing it well into the gashes. Cover and chill in the refrigerator for 24 hours.

Preheat the oven to fairly hot 200°C (Gas Mark 6, 400°F).

Put the chicken, on its back, on a rack in a roasting pan. Pour in enough water just to cover the bottom of the pan (to prevent the drippings from burning). Spoon the marinade in the bowl over the chicken, then a tablespoon of the melted butter. Roast for 1 hour, or until it is cooked through and tender, basting frequently with the remaining melted butter and the pan drippings. Remove from the oven.

Transfer the chicken to a carving board and carve into serving pieces. Arrange them on a warmed serving dish and spoon the drippings over. Serve at once. *Serves 3*
Preparation and cooking time: 26 hours

Madras Chicken Curry

Metric/Imperial	American
50ml./2fl.oz. vegetable oil	¼ cup vegetable oil
1 tsp. mustard seeds	1 tsp. mustard seeds
2 medium onions, finely chopped	2 medium onions, finely chopped
2½ cm./1in. piece of fresh root ginger, peeled and chopped	1in. piece of fresh green ginger, peeled and chopped
3 garlic cloves, crushed	3 garlic cloves, crushed
2 tsp. turmeric	2 tsp. turmeric

Metric/Imperial	American
1 Tbs. ground coriander	1 Tbs. ground coriander
1 tsp. hot chilli powder	1 tsp. hot chilli powder
¼ tsp. ground fenugreek	¼ tsp. ground fenugreek
2 tsp. ground cumin	2 tsp. ground cumin
1 tsp. black pepper	1 tsp. black pepper
8 chicken pieces, skinned	8 chicken pieces, skinned
600ml./1 pint coconut milk	2½ cups coconut milk
1 tsp. salt	1 tsp. salt
2 bay leaves	2 bay leaves
3 green chillis, slit lengthways and seeded	3 green chillis, slit lengthways and seeded
juice of ½ lemon	juice of ½ lemon

Heat the oil in a large saucepan. When it is hot, add the mustard seeds and fry until they begin to spatter. Add the onions, ginger and garlic and fry, stirring occasionally, until the onions are soft. Stir in the spices and fry for 5 minutes, stirring frequently. Add a tablespoonful or two of water if too dry.

Add the chicken pieces to the pan and turn them over to coat them thoroughly in the spices. Fry until they are evenly browned. Add all the remaining ingredients, except the lemon juice, and bring to the boil, stirring occasionally. Cover the pan, reduce the heat to low and simmer for 50 minutes, or until the chicken is cooked through and tender. After 30 minutes, uncover the pan and, if the curry is too liquid, simmer uncovered until it thickens. Stir in the lemon juice.

Remove from the heat and discard the bay leaves. Transfer to a warmed serving dish and serve at once.

Serves 4-6
Preparation and cooking time: 1¼ hours

Murg Kashmiri

(Chicken with Almonds and Raisins)

Metric/Imperial	American
1 x 2kg./4lb. chicken, skinned	1 x 4lb. chicken, skinned
juice of ½ lemon	juice of ½ lemon
1 Tbs. coriander seeds	1 Tbs. coriander seeds
1 tsp. black peppercorns	1 tsp. black peppercorns
1 tsp. cardamom seeds	1 tsp. cardamom seeds
6 cloves	6 cloves
4cm./1½in. piece of fresh root ginger, peeled and chopped	1½in. piece of fresh green ginger, peeled and chopped
1 tsp. salt	1 tsp. salt
½ tsp. hot chilli powder	½ tsp. hot chilli powder
75g./3oz. butter	6 Tbs. butter
2 medium onions, chopped	2 medium onions, chopped
300ml./10fl.oz. double cream	1¼ cups heavy cream
¼ tsp. saffron threads, soaked in 2 Tbs. boiling water	¼ tsp. saffron threads, soaked in 2 Tbs. boiling water
50g./2oz. slivered almonds	⅓ cup slivered almonds
50g./2oz. raisins	⅓ cup raisins

Preheat the oven to fairly hot 200°C (Gas Mark 6, 400°F). Prick the chicken all over, then rub over the lemon juice.

Put the spices into a mortar and grind coarsely with a pestle. Strain, discarding any husks left in the strainer, then mix in the ginger, salt and chilli powder. Cream half the butter to make a smooth paste, then beat into the spice mixture. Rub all over the chicken. Put the chicken into a flameproof casserole and put the casserole into the oven. Roast for 15 minutes.

Meanwhile, melt the remaining butter in a saucepan. Add the onions and fry, stirring occasionally, until they are golden brown. Remove from the heat and stir in the cream, saffron mixture, almonds and raisins.

Reduce the oven to moderate 180°C (Gas Mark 4, 350°F). Roast the chicken for 1 hour, or until it is cooked through, basting it every 10 minutes with the cream and almond mixture. Remove from the oven.

Transfer the chicken to a carving board and carve into serving pieces. Arrange the pieces in a warmed serving dish and keep hot.

Skim off most of the fat from the surface of the cooking liquid and set the casserole over moderate heat. Cook the sauce for 2 minutes, stirring constantly. Pour the sauce over the chicken pieces and serve at once.

Serves 4

Preparation and cooking time: 1½ hours

Sindhi Chicken

Metric/Imperial	American
1 x 2kg./4lb. chicken, skinned	1 x 4lb. chicken, skinned
1½ tsp. salt	1½ tsp. salt
1 tsp. bicarbonate of soda	1 tsp. baking soda
75g./3oz. butter	6 Tbs. butter
STUFFING	STUFFING
40g.1½/oz. cooked rice	½ cup cooked rice
2 large tomatoes, blanched, peeled, seeded and chopped	2 large tomatoes, blanched, peeled, seeded and chopped
1 large onion, chopped	1 large onion, chopped
1cm./½in. piece of fresh root ginger, peeled and chopped	½in. piece of fresh green ginger, peeled and chopped
1 green chilli, chopped	1 green chilli, chopped
salt and pepper	salt and pepper
1 hard-boiled egg, chopped	1 hard-boiled egg, chopped
50ml./2fl.oz. yogurt	¼ cup yogurt
25g./1oz. butter, melted	2 Tbs. butter, melted

Rub the chicken all over with the salt and soda. Set aside for 1 hour. Wash the chicken, then dry on kitchen towels.

Preheat the oven to moderate 180°C (Gas Mark 4, 350°F).

Melt 25g./1oz. (2 tablespoons) of butter in a deep frying-pan. Add the chicken and fry until it is evenly browned. Remove the pan from the heat and set the chicken aside until is it cool enough to handle.

Meanwhile, prepare the stuffing. Combine all the ingredients and mix well. Spoon into the cavity of the chicken and close with a skewer or a trussing needle and thread.

Put the chicken in an ovenproof dish. Cut the remaining butter into small pieces and scatter over the chicken. Put into the oven and roast for 1¼ hours, basting the chicken regularly with the butter. Remove from the oven.

Transfer the chicken to a carving board and carve into serving pieces. Arrange in a warmed serving dish, with the stuffing and cooking juices, and serve at once.

Serves 4

Preparation and cooking time: 2½ hours

Chicken Pulao

(Curried Rice with Chicken)

Metric/Imperial	American
50g./2oz. ghee or clarified butter	4 Tbs. ghee or clarified butter
1 large onion, sliced	1 large onion, sliced
2½cm./1in. piece of fresh root ginger, peeled and chopped	1in. piece of fresh green ginger, peeled and chopped
2 garlic cloves, crushed	2 garlic cloves, crushed
2 green chillis, chopped	2 green chillis, chopped
1 x 1½kg./3lb. chicken, cut into small serving pieces	1 x 3lb. chicken, cut into small serving pieces
1 tsp. turmeric	1 tsp. turmeric
½ tsp. hot chilli powder	½ tsp. hot chilli powder
1 Tbs. ground coriander	1 Tbs. ground coriander
1½tsp. salt	1½ tsp. salt
½ tsp. black pepper	½ tsp. black pepper
150ml./5fl.oz. yogurt	⅔ cup yogurt
juice of 1 small lemon	juice of 1 small lemon
350g./12oz. long-grain rice, soaked in cold water for 30 minutes and drained	2 cups long-grain rice, soaked in cold water for 30 minutes and drained
400ml./12fl.oz. boiling water	1½ cups boiling water

Melt the ghee or clarified butter in a saucepan. Add the onion and fry, stirring occasionally, until it is soft. Add the ginger, garlic and chillis and fry for 4 minutes, stirring occasionally. Add the chicken pieces and fry until they are evenly browned.

Combine the spices, salt, pepper, yogurt and lemon juice, then stir the mixture into the pan. Cover, reduce the heat to low and simmer for 40 minutes, or until the chicken is cooked through and tender. Uncover and stir in the rice and cook until most of the liquid has been absorbed. Pour over the water and cover the pan. Reduce the heat to low and simmer the pulau for 15 to 20 minutes, or until the rice is cooked and the liquid absorbed.

Serve at once.

Serves 4
Preparation and cooking time: 1¾ hours

White Chicken Curry

Metric/Imperial	American
1 cinnamon stick	1 cinnamon stick
2 tsp. cardamom seeds	2 tsp. cardamom seeds
4 peppercorns	4 peppercorns
4 cloves	4 cloves
50g./2oz. butter	4 Tbs. butter
3 garlic cloves, crushed	3 garlic cloves, crushed
5cm./2in. piece of fresh root ginger, peeled and chopped	2in. piece of fresh green ginger, peeled and chopped
4 medium onions, chopped	4 medium onions, chopped

1 x 2kg./4lb. chicken, cut into serving
   pieces
450ml./15fl.oz. yogurt
1 tsp. hot chilli powder
1 tsp. salt
¼ tsp. saffron threads, soaked in
   2 Tbs. boiling water
250ml./8fl.oz. thick coconut milk
3 Tbs. ground almonds

1 x 4lb. chicken, cut into serving
   pieces
2 cups yogurt
1 tsp. hot chilli powder
1 tsp. salt
¼ tsp. saffron threads, soaked in
   2 Tbs. boiling water
1 cup thick coconut milk
3 Tbs. ground almonds

Put the spices and peppercorns in a blender and blend to a powder. Set aside.

Melt the butter in a saucepan. Add the spice powder and fry for 1 minute, stirring constantly. Add the garlic, ginger and onions and fry, stirring frequently, until the onions are golden brown. Add the chicken pieces and fry until they are evenly browned.

Meanwhile, combine the yogurt with the chilli powder, salt and saffron mixture, then pour into the pan. Bring to the boil, cover the pan and reduce the heat to low. Simmer for 30 minutes. Stir in the coconut milk and ground almonds and bring to the boil again. Reduce the heat to low and simmer, uncovered, for 30 minutes, or until the chicken is cooked through and tender. (If the sauce is too thin, remove the chicken from the pan and boil the sauce for 10 to 15 minutes or until it thickens.)

Transfer the curry and chicken to a warmed serving dish and serve at once.

Serves 4
Preparation and cooking time: 1¾ hours

White Chicken Curry, accompanied by rice, chutneys and poppadums, makes a delicately flavoured dish.

Dhansak

(Chicken with Dhal [Lentils] and Vegetables)

Metric/Imperial	American
125g./4oz. tur dhal	½ cup tur dhal
25g./1oz. channa dhal	2 Tbs. channa dhal
50g./2oz. masoor dhal	¼ cup masoor dhal
25g./1oz. moong dhal	2 Tbs. moong dhal
900ml./1½ pints water	3¾ cups water
2 tsp. salt	2 tsp. salt
40g./1½oz. ghee or clarified butter	3 Tbs. ghee or clarified butter
2½cm./1in. piece of fresh root ginger, peeled and chopped	1in. piece of fresh green ginger, peeled and chopped
1 garlic clove, crushed	1 garlic clove, crushed
8 chicken pieces	8 chicken pieces
1 Tbs. chopped fresh mint	1 Tbs. chopped fresh mint
225g./8oz. aubergines, cubed	1 cup cubed eggplants
225g./8oz. pumpkin, cubed	1 cup cubed pumpkin
125g./4oz. chopped spinach	⅔ cup chopped spinach
1 large onion, sliced	1 large onion, sliced
½kg./1lb. tomatoes, blanched, peeled and chopped	1lb. tomatoes, blanched, peeled and chopped
MASALA	MASALA
50g./2oz. ghee or clarified butter	4 Tbs. ghee or clarified butter
1 large onion, sliced	1 large onion, sliced
4cm./1½in. piece of fresh root ginger, peeled and chopped	1½in. piece of fresh green ginger, peeled and chopped
3 green chillis, chopped	3 green chillis, chopped
3 garlic cloves, crushed	3 garlic cloves, crushed
½ tsp. ground cinnamon	½ tsp. ground cinnamon
½ tsp. ground cardamom	½ tsp. ground cardamom
½ tsp. ground cloves	½ tsp. ground cloves
1½ tsp. turmeric	1½ tsp. turmeric
1 tsp. ground coriander	1 tsp. ground coriander
¼ tsp. hot chilli powder	¼ tsp. hot chilli powder
3 Tbs. chopped coriander leaves	3 Tbs. chopped coriander leaves

Wash all the dhals (lentils) thoroughly in cold running water and soak for 30 minutes. Drain and transfer them to a saucepan. Add the water and salt and bring to the boil, skimming off any scum that rises to the surface. Cover the pan, reduce the heat to low and simmer for 40 minutes.

Meanwhile, melt the ghee or clarified butter in a large frying-pan. Add the ginger and garlic and fry for 2 minutes, stirring frequently. Add the chicken pieces and fry until they are evenly browned.

Transfer the chicken mixture to the dhal, then stir in the vegetables and tomatoes. Bring to the boil, reduce the heat to low and simmer for 45 minutes, or until the chicken is cooked through and tender.

Transfer the chicken to a plate. Purée the vegetables and dhal in a blender and set aside.

Rinse and dry the saucepan. To make the masala, melt the ghee or clarified butter in the saucepan. Add the onion and fry, stirring occasionally, until it is golden brown. Add the ginger, chillis and garlic and fry for 3 minutes, stirring frequently. Add all the remaining ingredients, except the coriander leaves, and fry for 8 minutes, stirring constantly. Add a spoonful or two of water if the mixture becomes too dry.

Stir the puréed vegetables and dhal into the pan and bring to the boil. Cover the pan, reduce the heat to low and simmer for 20 minutes. Stir in the chicken pieces and baste well with the sauce. Simmer for 10 minutes, or until they are heated through.

Transfer the dhansak to a warmed serving dish and sprinkle over the coriander before serving.

Serves 6
Preparation and cooking time: 3 hours

(See over) Dhansak com- bines chicken, lentils and vegetables to produce a delicious and filling meal.

Spiced Almond Chicken

Metric/Imperial	American
1 x 2kg./4lb. chicken	1 x 4lb. chicken
juice of 1½ lemons	juice of 1½ lemons
2 tsp. salt	2 tsp. salt
1 tsp. cayenne pepper	1 tsp. cayenne pepper
¼ tsp. saffron threads, soaked in 2 Tbs. boiling water for 10 minutes	¼ tsp. saffron threads, soaked in 2 Tbs. boiling water for 10 minutes
50g./2oz. butter, melted	4 Tbs. butter, melted
MARINADE	MARINADE
50g./2oz. raisins	⅓ cup raisins
75g./3oz. flaked almonds	½ cup slivered almonds
1 Tbs. clear honey	1 Tbs. clear honey
2 garlic cloves	2 garlic cloves
5cm./2in. piece of fresh root ginger, peeled and chopped	5cm./2in. piece of fresh green ginger, peeled and chopped
½ tsp. cardamom seeds	½ tsp. cardamom seeds
½ tsp. cumin seeds	½ tsp. cumin seeds
1 tsp. turmeric	1 tsp. turmeric
150ml./5fl.oz. yogurt	⅔ cup yogurt
125ml./4fl.oz. double cream	½ cup heavy cream

Make diagonal slits in the breast and thighs of the chicken. Combine the lemon juice, salt and cayenne then rub the mixture all over the chicken, especially into the slits. Put the chicken into a large bowl and set aside for 30 minutes.

Meanwhile, make the marinade. Put the raisins, almonds, honey, garlic, ginger and spices into a blender with 4 tablespoons of yogurt and blend to a smooth purée.

Transfer the purée to a bowl and beat in the remaining yogurt and the cream. Pour over the chicken, cover the bowl and chill in the refrigerator for 24 hours, turning occasionally. Remove from the refrigerator and set aside at room temperature for 1 hour.

Preheat the oven to fairly hot 200°C (Gas Mark 6, 400°F).

Put the chicken into a deep roasting pan. Combine the saffron mixture with the remaining marinade and pour over the chicken. Spoon a little of the melted butter over the top. Pour 150ml./5fl.oz. (⅔ cup) of water into the roasting pan and put the pan into the oven. Roast the chicken for 1 hour, or until it is cooked through and tender, basting frequently with the remaining melted butter and the liquid in the tin. Remove from the oven.

Transfer the chicken to a warmed serving dish. Spoon the tin juices over the chicken and serve at once.

Serves 4
Preparation and cooking time: 26 hours

Goan Vinegar Curry is a very spicy and hot chicken dish from the west coast of India.

Goan Vinegar Curry

Metric/Imperial	American
75ml./3fl.oz. vegetable oil	$\frac{3}{4}$ cup vegetable oil
5cm./2in. piece of fresh root ginger, peeled and chopped	3in. piece of fresh root ginger, peeled and chopped
3 green chillis, chopped	3 green chillis, chopped
3 garlic cloves, crushed	3 garlic cloves, crushed
1 x 2kg./4lb. chicken, cut into serving pieces	1 x 4lb. chicken, cut into serving pieces
$\frac{1}{2}$ tsp. ground cardamom	$\frac{1}{2}$ tsp. ground cardamom
$\frac{1}{2}$ tsp. ground cloves	$\frac{1}{2}$ tsp. ground cloves
$\frac{1}{2}$ tsp. ground cinnamon	$\frac{1}{2}$ tsp. ground cinnamon
$1\frac{1}{2}$ tsp. turmeric	$1\frac{1}{2}$ tsp. turmeric
1 Tbs. ground coriander	1 Tbs. ground coriander
1 tsp. hot chilli powder	1 tsp. hot chilli powder
250ml./8fl.oz. vinegar	1 cup vinegar
4 large onions, sliced	4 large onions, sliced
150ml./5fl.oz. water	$\frac{5}{8}$ cup water
1 tsp. salt	1 tsp. salt

Heat the oil in a saucepan. When it is hot, add the ginger, chillis and garlic and fry for 2 minutes, stirring frequently. Add the chicken pieces and fry until they are evenly browned. Transfer the chicken to a plate.

Mix the spices with enough vinegar to make a smooth paste. Set aside.

Add the onions to the pan and fry, stirring occasionally, until they are golden brown. Add the spice paste and fry for 8 minutes, stirring frequently. Add a spoonful or two of water if the mixture becomes too dry.

Return the chicken pieces to the pan and pour in the remaining vinegar, the water and salt. Bring to the boil, cover the pan and reduce the heat to low. Simmer for 1 hour, or until the chicken is cooked through and tender.

Transfer the mixture to a warmed serving dish and serve at once.

Serves 4
Preparation and cooking time: 1¾ hours

Dopeeazah Chicken

(Chicken with Onions)

Metric/Imperial	American
1 x 2kg./4lb. chicken, skinned and cut into serving pieces	1 x 4lb. chicken, skinned and cut into serving pieces
1 tsp. salt	1 tsp. salt
50g./2oz. butter	4 Tbs. butter
1kg./2lb. onions, chopped	2lb. onions, chopped
2 garlic cloves, crushed	2 garlic cloves, crushed
5cm./2in. piece of fresh root ginger, peeled and chopped	2in. piece of fresh green ginger, peeled and chopped
1 green chilli, chopped	1 green chilli, chopped
½ tsp. cardamom seeds	½ tsp. cardamom seeds
1 tsp. turmeric	1 tsp. turmeric
1½ tsp. ground cumin	1½ tsp. ground cumin
1 tsp. ground coriander	1 tsp. ground coriander
450ml./15fl.oz. yogurt	2 cups yogurt
½ tsp. saffron threads, soaked in 2 Tbs. boiling water	½ tsp. saffron threads, soaked in 2 Tbs. boiling water
10 peppercorns	10 peppercorns

Preheat the oven to warm 170°C (Gas Mark 3, 325°F).

Rub the chicken pieces with salt and set aside. Melt the butter in a flameproof casserole. Add half the onions and fry, stirring occasionally, until they are soft. Add the garlic, ginger and chilli. Transfer the mixture to a bowl, draining off as much cooking liquid as possible.

Add the chicken pieces, cardamom, spices, yogurt and saffron mixture to the casserole and bring to the boil. Mash the cooked onion mixture to a pulp and return to the casserole. Arrange the uncooked onions and peppercorns on top. Cover the casserole and transfer to the oven. Bake for 1½ hours, or until the chicken is cooked through and tender.

Serve at once, straight from the casserole.

Serves 6
Preparation and cooking time: 2 hours

Kukul Murg

(Sri Lankan Chicken Curry)

Metric/Imperial	American
50g./2oz. ghee or clarified butter	4 Tbs. ghee or clarified butter
2 medium onions, chopped	2 medium onions, chopped

Metric/Imperial	American
3 garlic cloves, crushed	3 garlic cloves, crushed
2.5cm./1in. piece of fresh root ginger, peeled and chopped	1in. piece of fresh green ginger, peeled and chopped
$\frac{1}{2}$ tsp. crushed fenugreek seeds	$\frac{1}{2}$ tsp. crushed fenugreek seeds
5 curry or bay leaves	5 curry or bay leaves
1 tsp. turmeric	1 tsp. turmeric
1 tsp. hot chilli powder	1 tsp. hot chilli powder
2 tsp. ground coriander	2 tsp. ground coriander
1 tsp. ground cumin	1 tsp. ground cumin
$\frac{1}{2}$ tsp. ground cardamom	$\frac{1}{2}$ tsp. ground cardamom
2 Tbs. vinegar	2 Tbs. vinegar
1 tsp. salt	1 tsp. salt
1 x 2kg./4lb. chicken, cut into serving pieces	1 x 4lb. chicken, cut into serving pieces
2 tomatoes, blanched, peeled and chopped	2 tomatoes, blanched, peeled and chopped
1 Tbs. tomato purée	1 Tbs. tomato paste
1 tsp. chopped lemon grass or grated lemon rind	1 tsp. chopped lemon grass or grated lemon rind
300ml./10fl.oz. thick coconut milk	$1\frac{1}{4}$ cups thick coconut milk

Melt the ghee in a large saucepan. Add the onions, garlic and ginger and fry, stirring occasionally, until the onions are soft. Add the fenugreek and curry or bay leaves and fry for 1 minute. Stir in the ground spices, vinegar and salt and fry for 5 minutes, stirring constantly. Add the chicken pieces and cook until they are evenly browned and coated with the spice mixture. Stir in the tomatoes, tomato purée (paste) and lemon grass or rind and cook for 3 minutes. Pour over the coconut milk and bring to the boil.

Reduce the heat to low, cover the pan and simmer the mixture for 45 minutes to 1 hour, or until the chicken is cooked through and tender.

Transfer the mixture to a warmed serving dish and serve at once.
Serves 4-6
Preparation and cooking time: $1\frac{1}{2}$ hours

Vath

(Roast Duck)

Metric/Imperial	American
1 x $2\frac{1}{2}$kg./5lb. duck, oven-ready	1 x 5lb. duck, oven-ready
2 tsp. salt	2 tsp. salt
juice of 1 lemon	juice of 1 lemon
4 garlic cloves, crushed	4 garlic cloves, crushed
2 tsp. turmeric	2 tsp. turmeric
1 Tbs. ground coriander	1 Tbs. ground coriander
1 Tbs. garam masala	1 Tbs. garam masala
2 tsp. ground cumin	2 tsp. ground cumin
4 green chillis, chopped	4 green chillis, chopped
125ml./4fl.oz. sour cream	$\frac{1}{2}$ cup sour cream
175g./6oz. roasted cashewnuts, coarsely chopped	1 cup roasted cashewnuts, coarsely chopped
125g./4oz. pork sausagemeat	4oz. pork sausagemeat

small oranges, peeled, pith and
seeds removed and chopped

2 small oranges, peeled, pith and
seeds removed and chopped

Rub the duck all over with 1½ teaspoons of salt.

Combine the lemon juice, half the garlic, spices, chillis and sour cream. Put the duck in a shallow dish and spoon over the spice mixture. Rub all over the duck and set aside to marinate for 2 hours at room temperature.

Preheat the oven to very hot 230°C (Gas Mark 8, 450°F).

Combine the remaining salt, garlic, spices and sour cream. Add the cashewnuts, sausagemeat and oranges and beat until the mixture is thoroughly blended. Remove the duck from the marinade and put on a working surface. Stir any marinade remaining into the stuffing mixture, then spoon into the duck cavity. Secure with skewers or a trussing needle and thread.

Put the duck on a rack in a roasting pan. Put the pan into the oven and roast for 15 minutes. Reduce the oven to moderate 180°C (Gas Mark 4, 350°F) and roast the duck for a further 1¼ hours, or until it is cooked through and tender. Remove from the oven.

Transfer to a carving board, cut into serving pieces and serve at once.

Serves 4

Preparation and cooking time: 4¾ hours

Vath is a splendid dish of roast duck, stuffed with a mixture of pork sausagemeat, oranges and cashew nuts.

Served with plain boiled rice, home-made chutney and a tomato and onion salad, Duck Curry will make a rich meal.

Duck Curry

Metric/Imperial	American
5 Tbs. vegetable oil	5 Tbs. vegetable oil
1 x 3kg./6lb. duck, cut into serving pieces	1 x 6lb. duck, cut into serving pieces
1 tsp. mustard seeds	1 tsp. mustard seeds
3 medium onions, chopped	3 medium onions, chopped
2 garlic cloves, finely chopped	2 garlic cloves, finely chopped
4cm./1½in. piece of fresh root ginger, peeled and chopped	1½in. piece of fresh green ginger, peeled and chopped
1 green chilli, finely chopped	1 green chilli, finely chopped
1 tsp. ground cumin	1 tsp. ground cumin
1 tsp. hot chilli powder	1 tsp. hot chilli powder
1 Tbs. ground coriander	1 Tbs. ground coriander
1 Tbs. garam masala	1 Tbs. garam masala
1 tsp. turmeric	1 tsp. turmeric
½ tsp. salt	½ tsp. salt
3 Tbs. vinegar	3 Tbs. vinegar
350ml./12fl.oz. coconut milk	1½ cups coconut milk

Heat the oil in a large saucepan. When it is hot, add the duck pieces and fry until they are evenly browned. Transfer to a plate. Add the mustard seeds and cover the pan. When they have stopped spattering, stir in the onions and fry, stirring occasionally, until they are golden brown. Add the garlic, ginger, and chilli and fry for 2 minutes, stirring frequently.

Put the spices and salt in a small bowl and mix to a smooth paste with the vinegar. Stir into the saucepan and fry for 5 to 8 minutes, stirring constantly. Add the duck pieces and turn in the paste to coat them thoroughly. Fry for a further 3 minutes.

Pour over the coconut milk and bring to the boil. Cover the pan, reduce the heat to low and simmer for 1 hour, or until the duck is cooked through and tender and the gravy is thick.

Transfer to a warmed serving dish and serve at once.

Serves 4-5
Preparation and cooking time: 1½ hours

Curried Partridges

Metric/Imperial	American
4 partridges, oven-ready with the giblets reserved	4 partridges, oven-ready with the giblets reserved
1½ tsp. salt	1½ tsp. salt
900ml./1½ pints water	3¾ cups water
4 cloves	4 cloves
2½cm./1in. piece of fresh root ginger, peeled and chopped	1in. piece of fresh green ginger, peeled and chopped
4 garlic cloves, chopped	4 garlic cloves, chopped
1 onion, halved	1 onion, halved
50g./2oz. butter	4 Tbs. butter
3 medium onions, finely chopped	3 medium onions, finely chopped
2 tsp. ground coriander	2 tsp. ground coriander
1 tsp. cayenne pepper	1 tsp. cayenne pepper
300ml./10fl.oz. single cream	1¼ cups light cream
125g./4oz. ground almonds	⅔ cup ground almonds
1 tsp. crushed cardamom seeds	1 tsp. crushed cardamom seeds
¼ tsp. saffron threads, soaked in 2 Tbs. boiling water	¼ tsp. saffron threads, soaked in 2 Tbs. boiling water

Mix the lemon juice with 1 teaspoon of salt and rub all over the partridges. Set aside while you make the stock.

Put the giblets, water, spices and halved onion into a saucepan and bring to the boil. Cover the pan, reduce the heat to low and simmer for 1½ hours. Remove from the heat and strain the stock into a bowl. Rinse and dry the pan. Return the strained stock to the pan and bring to the boil. Boil until the stock reduces to about 300ml./10fl.oz. (1¼ cups).

Melt the butter in a flameproof casserole. Add the chopped onions and fry, stirring occasionally, until they are golden brown. Stir in the coriander and cayenne and fry for 3 minutes, stirring frequently. Add the partridges and fry until they are evenly browned. Pour over the reserved stock and the remaining salt and bring to the boil. Cover, reduce the heat to low and simmer for 20 minutes. Uncover and continue simmering for a further 30 to 35 minutes, or until the partridges are cooked through and tender and the liquid has evaporated.

Preheat the oven to cool 150°C (Gas Mark 2, 300°F).

Mix the cream, almonds, cardamom and saffron mixture together and pour over the partridges. Bring to the boil, cover and transfer to the oven. Bake for 20 minutes. Remove from the oven and serve at once, straight from the casserole.

Serves 4
Preparation and cooking time: 3 hours

FISH & SEAFOOD

Sondhia

(Spiced Prawns or Shrimps)

Metric/Imperial	American
1kg./2lb. uncooked Dublin Bay Prawns	2lb. uncooked large Gulf shrimps
1 tsp. hot chilli powder	1 tsp. hot chilli powder
1 tsp. ground cumin	1 tsp. ground cumin
2 tsp. turmeric	2 tsp. turmeric
1½ tsp. salt	1½ tsp. salt
3 garlic cloves, crushed	3 garlic cloves, crushed
3 green chillis, chopped	3 green chillis, chopped
50ml./2fl.oz. lemon juice	¼ cup lemon juice
300ml./10fl.oz. water	1¼ cups water
50ml./2fl.oz. vegetable oil	¼ cup vegetable oil
2 Tbs. chopped coriander leaves	2 Tbs. chopped coriander leaves

Shell the prawns (shrimps) and reserve the shells. Devein the prawns (shrimps) and wash under cold running water. Dry and transfer to a large bowl.

Combine the spices, salt, garlic and chillis with just enough of the lemon juice to make a paste. Rub the paste into the prawns (shrimps) and set aside for 1 hour.

Meanwhile, put the raw (shrimp) shells into a saucepan and pour over the water. Bring to the boil, cover and reduce the heat to low. Simmer for 20 minutes, then strain the stock into a jug, reserving about 250ml./8fl.oz. (1 cup).

Heat the oil in a large frying-pan. When it is hot, add the prawns (shrimps) and simmer for 5 minutes, or until they turn evenly pink. Stir in the reserved stock, and bring to the boil. Reduce the heat to low and simmer for 20 minutes, or until the prawns (shrimps) are cooked and tender. Stir in the remaining lemon juice and coriander leaves. Remove from the heat.

Transfer to a warmed serving dish and serve at once.
Serves 4-6
Preparation and cooking time: 2 hours

Jhinga Pakoras

(Shrimp and Chick-Pea Fritters)

Metric/Imperial	American
125g./4oz. chick-pea flour	1 cup chick-pea flour
½ tsp. hot chilli powder	½ tsp. hot chilli powder
½ tsp. salt	½ tsp. salt
¼ tsp. turmeric	¼ tsp. turmeric
250-300ml./8-10fl.oz. water	1-1¼ cups water
350g./12oz. shelled shrimps	12oz. shelled shrimps
vegetable oil for deep-frying	vegetable oil for deep-frying

Sondhia, an exotic blend of prawns or shrimps and spices, makes an appetizing main course.

Sift the flour and spices into a bowl. Make a well in the centre and pour in enough of the water to beat to a smooth batter, the consistency of thick cream. (If the

batter is too thick, add more water.) Cover and set aside to 'rest' at room temperature for 30 minutes. Just before frying, mix in the shrimps.

Fill a large deep-frying pan one-third full with oil and heat until it is hot. Drop tablespoonfuls of the batter into the oil and fry for 4 minutes, or until they are crisp and golden brown. As they cook, transfer them to kitchen towels to drain.

Serve hot.

Serves 4
Preparation and cooking time: 50 minutes

Jhinga Kari I

(Prawn or Shrimp Curry)

Jinga Kari I, a colourful and tasty way of cooking prawns or shrimps, is very palatable served with boiled rice and Chapatti.

Metric/Imperial	American
4cm./1½in. piece of fresh root ginger, peeled and chopped	1½in. piece of fresh green ginger, peeled and chopped
3 garlic cloves	3 garlic cloves
4 green chillis, seeded	4 green chillis, seeded
6 Tbs. chopped coriander leaves	6 Tbs. chopped coriander leaves

82

Metric/Imperial	American
Tbs. coriander seeds	1 Tbs. coriander seeds
juice of 1 lemon	juice of 1 lemon
450ml./15fl.oz. thick coconut milk	2 cups thick coconut milk
75ml./3fl.oz. vegetable oil	$\frac{1}{3}$ cup vegetable oil
700g./1½lb. large prawns, shelled	1½lb. large shrimps, shelled
2 medium onions, chopped	2 medium onions, chopped
1 tsp. turmeric	1 tsp. turmeric
1 tsp. mustard seeds	1 tsp. mustard seeds
1 tsp. salt	1 tsp. salt

Put the ginger, garlic, chillis, coriander leaves and seeds into a blender with the lemon juice and 4 tablespoons of coconut milk. Blend to form a thick paste, adding more milk if necessary. Transfer the paste to a small bowl.

Heat 50ml./2fl.oz. (¼ cup) of oil in a large saucepan. When it is hot, add the prawns or shrimps and fry, turning frequently, for 5 minutes. Transfer to a plate and set aside.

Add the remaining oil to the pan. Add the onions and fry until they are golden. Stir in the turmeric, mustard seeds and salt and fry for 1 minute, stirring constantly. Add the spice paste and fry for 5 minutes, stirring constantly. Return the prawns or shrimps to the pan and coat them thoroughly in the paste. Pour in the remaining coconut milk and bring to the boil. Cover the pan, reduce the heat to low and simmer for 30 minutes.

Transfer the curry to a warmed serving bowl and serve at once.
Serves 4-6
Preparation and cooking time: 50 minutes

Jhinga Kari II

(Prawn or Shrimp Curry)

Metric/Imperial	American
50g./2oz. butter	4 Tbs. butter
1 medium onion, chopped	1 medium onion, chopped
2 garlic cloves, crushed	2 garlic cloves, crushed
2½cm./1in. piece of fresh root ginger, peeled and chopped	1in. piece of fresh green ginger, peeled and chopped
1kg./2lb. Dublin Bay prawns, shelled	2lb. large Gulf shrimps, shelled
1 tsp. turmeric	1 tsp. turmeric
1 tsp. hot chilli powder	1 tsp. hot chilli powder
1 Tbs. ground coriander	1 Tbs. ground coriander
1 tsp. ground cumin	1 tsp. ground cumin
1 tsp. salt	1 tsp. salt
½ tsp. black pepper	½ tsp. black pepper
150ml./5fl.oz. yogurt or sour cream	$\frac{2}{3}$ cup yogurt or sour cream

Melt the butter in a saucepan. Add the onion, garlic and ginger and fry, stirring occasionally, until the onion is golden brown. Add the prawns or shrimps and fry for 5 minutes, stirring occasionally. Stir in the spices, seasoning and yogurt or cream. Bring to the boil, reduce the heat to low and simmer for 30 minutes, stirring frequently, or until the sauce has thickened.

Transfer the mixture to a warmed serving dish and serve at once.
Serves 6
Preparation and cooking time: 1 hour

Jhinga Kari III

(Prawn or Shrimp Curry)

Metric/Imperial	American
50ml./2fl.oz. vegetable oil	$\frac{1}{4}$ cup vegetable oil
4cm./1$\frac{1}{2}$in. piece of fresh root ginger, peeled and chopped	1$\frac{1}{2}$in. piece of fresh green ginger, peeled and chopped
2 garlic cloves, crushed	2 garlic cloves, crushed
2 large onions, finely chopped	2 large onions, chopped
3 green chillis, finely chopped	3 green chillis, finely chopped
2 Tbs. ground coriander	2 Tbs. ground coriander
2 tsp. turmeric	2 tsp. turmeric
3 Tbs. wine vinegar	3 Tbs. wine vinegar
1 tsp. salt	1 tsp. salt
1kg./2lb. large cooked prawns, shelled	2lb. large cooked shrimps, peeled
450ml./15fl.oz. hot coconut milk	2 cups hot coconut milk

Heat the oil in a large saucepan. When it is hot, add the ginger and garlic and fry for 1 minute, stirring constantly. Add the onions and fry until they are golden brown. Stir in the chillis and fry for 30 seconds. Stir in the spices, reduce the heat to low and simmer for 4 minutes, stirring constantly. Stir in the vinegar and salt and fry for 30 seconds.

Stir in the prawns (shrimps) and fry for 2 to 3 minutes, tossing until they are completely coated in the spices. Pour over the milk and bring to the boil. Cover the pan, reduce the heat to low and simmer for 5 minutes.

Transfer to a warmed serving dish and serve at once.

Serves 6
Preparation and cooking time: 30 minutes

Jhinga Tikka

(Prawn or Shrimp Patties)

Metric/Imperial	American
275g./10oz. prawns, shelled	10oz. shrimp, shelled
1 medium onion	1 medium onion
1cm./$\frac{1}{2}$in. piece of fresh root ginger, peeled	$\frac{1}{2}$in. piece of fresh green ginger, peeled
1 green chilli	1 green chilli
1 Tbs. chopped coriander leaves	1 Tbs. chopped coriander leaves
$\frac{3}{4}$ tsp. salt	$\frac{3}{4}$ tsp. salt
1 Tbs. lemon juice	1 Tbs. lemon juice
2 Tbs. fresh white breadcrumbs	2 Tbs. fresh white breadcrumbs
$\frac{1}{4}$ tsp. turmeric	$\frac{1}{4}$ tsp. turmeric
$\frac{1}{4}$ tsp. black pepper	$\frac{1}{4}$ tsp. black pepper
1 egg	1 egg
75g./3oz. dry breadcrumbs	1 cup dry breadcrumbs
50ml./2fl.oz. vegetable oil	$\frac{1}{4}$ cup vegetable oil

Finely chop the prawns (shrimp), onion, ginger and chilli and put into a bowl. Mix in the coriander, salt, lemon juice, breadcrumbs, turmeric, pepper and the egg. Knead to blend thoroughly. Divide into eight equal portions and shape them into flat round patties. Dip the patties into the dry breadcrumbs to coat them thoroughly.

Heat the oil in a large frying-pan. When it is hot, add the patties and fry for 5 to 7 minutes on each side, or until they are golden brown.

Transfer to a warmed serving dish and serve at once.

Serves 4
Preparation and cooking time: 30 minutes

Shrimp Pulao

(Curried Rice with Shrimps)

Metric/Imperial	American
½kg./1lb. uncooked prawns, shelled	1lb. uncooked shrimps, shelled
1½ tsp. salt	1½ tsp. salt
½ tsp. cayenne pepper	½ tsp. cayenne pepper
juice of ½ lemon	juice of ½ lemon
40g./1½oz. butter	3 Tbs. butter
2 medium onions, sliced	2 medium onions, sliced
2 garlic cloves, crushed	2 garlic cloves, crushed
1 tsp. cumin seeds	1 tsp. cumin seeds
1 tsp. turmeric	1 tsp. turmeric
125g./4oz. French beans, sliced	⅔ cup sliced green beans
3 carrots, sliced	3 carrots, sliced
2 small courgettes, sliced	2 small zucchini, sliced
350g./12oz. long-grain rice, soaked in cold water for 30 minutes and drained	2 cups long-grain rice, soaked in cold water for 30 minutes and drained
SAUCE	SAUCE
2 Tbs. vegetable oil	2 Tbs. vegetable oil
1 medium onion, chopped	1 medium onion, chopped
1 garlic clove, crushed	1 garlic clove, crushed
4cm./1½in. piece of fresh root ginger, peeled and chopped	1½in. piece of fresh green ginger, peeled and chopped
2 green chillis, chopped	2 green chillis, chopped
1 tsp. turmeric	1 tsp. turmeric
1 Tbs. ground coriander	1 Tbs. ground coriander
½ tsp. cayenne pepper	½ tsp. cayenne pepper
2 tsp. paprika	2 tsp. paprika
700g./1½lb. canned peeled tomatoes rubbed through a sieve with the can juice	1½lb. canned peeled tomatoes, rubbed through a strainer with the can juice
1 tsp. sugar	1 tsp. sugar
1 tsp. salt	1 tsp. salt
4cm./1½in. slice creamed coconut	1½in. slice creamed coconut

Put the prawns or shrimps on a plate and rub them all over with ½ teaspoon of salt, the cayenne and lemon juice. Set aside for 30 minutes.

Meanwhile, make the sauce. Heat the oil in a saucepan. When it is hot, add the onion, garlic, ginger and chillis and fry, stirring occasionally, until the onion is golden brown. Stir in the spices and fry for 2 minutes, then stir in the strained tomatoes, sugar and salt. Bring to the boil, cover and reduce the heat to low. Simmer for 20 minutes. Stir in the creamed coconut and bring to the boil again when it has dissolved. Cover and simmer for a further 20 minutes.

Meanwhile, melt the butter in a large saucepan. Add the prawns or shrimps and fry for 5 minutes, or until they become slightly pink. Transfer to a plate

A wide variety of accompaniments, such as Poppadums, chutneys and salads, are suitable to serve with Shrimp Pulao, a tasty combination of curried rice with shrimps.

and set aside.

Add the onions and garlic to the pan and fry, stirring occasionally, until the onions are golden brown. Stir in the cumin and turmeric and add the vegetables. Cover the pan, reduce the heat to low and simmer for 10 minutes. Stir in the rice and remaining salt and fry for 2 minutes, stirring constantly. Return the prawns or shrimps to the pan and pour in enough boiling water to cover by about 1cm./½in. When the liquid is boiling vigorously, cover the pan, reduce the heat to low and simmer for 15 to 20 minutes, or until the rice is cooked and the liquid absorbed.

Remove from the heat and spoon the rice on to a warmed serving dish. Pour the sauce into a bowl and serve, with the rice.

Serves 4-6
Preparation and cooking time: 2½ hours

Bangra Masala

(Spiced Fish)

Metric/Imperial	American
4 herrings, cleaned and gutted	4 herrings, cleaned and gutted
2½ tsp. salt	2½ tsp. salt
juice of ½ lemon	juice of ½ lemon
3 Tbs. flour	3 Tbs. flour
1 tsp. turmeric	1 tsp. turmeric
4-6 Tbs. cooking oil	4-6 Tbs. cooking oil
FILLING	FILLING
3 Tbs. cooking oil	3 Tbs. cooking oil
2 small onions, minced	2 small onions, ground
1 tsp. turmeric	1 tsp. turmeric
1 tsp. ground coriander	1 tsp. ground coriander
1 tsp. hot chilli powder	1 tsp. hot chilli powder
1 Tbs. garam masala	1 Tbs. garam masala
1 large garlic clove, crushed	1 large garlic clove, crushed
4cm./1½in. piece of fresh root ginger, peeled and chopped	1½in. piece of fresh green ginger, peeled and chopped
juice of ½ lemon	juice of ½ lemon
75g./3oz. tomato purée	3oz. tomato paste

Sprinkle the inside of each fish with ½ teaspoon of salt and set aside.

To make the filling, heat the oil in a frying-pan. When it is hot, add the onions and fry, stirring occasionally, until they are golden brown. Add the spices and fry for 8 minutes, stirring occasionally. Add the garlic and ginger and fry for 2 minutes, stirring frequently. Add the spices and fry for 8 minutes, stirring constantly. Add a spoonful or two of water if the mixture becomes too dry. Stir in the lemon juice and tomato purée (paste) and cook for 3 minutes. Remove from the heat and divide the filling between the fish. Close the openings, then gash the sides of the fish with a sharp knife and rub in a little lemon juice. Mix the flour, turmeric and remaining salt on a plate, then dip the fish into the mixture, one by one.

Heat the oil in a large frying-pan. When it is hot, add the fish and fry for about 10 minutes, turning occasionally, or until the fish is cooked and flakes easily.

Serves 4
Preparation and cooking time: 45 minutes

Fish Molee

Any type of firm, white fish can be used in this recipe – cheaper fish such as coley and huss could be substituted for the whiting suggested below.

Metric/Imperial	American
3 Tbs. peanut oil	3 Tbs. peanut oil
2 garlic cloves, crushed	2 garlic cloves, crushed
8 shallots, peeled and chopped	8 shallots, peeled and chopped
2.5cm./1in. piece of fresh root ginger, peeled and chopped	1in piece of fresh green ginger, peeled and chopped
juice of 2 lemons	juice of 2 lemons
150ml./5fl.oz. water	⅔ cup water
grated rind of 1 lemon	grated rind of 1 lemon
1 red chilli, chopped	1 red chilli, chopped
1 tsp. turmeric	1 tsp. turmeric
300ml./10fl.oz. thin coconut milk	1¼ cups thin coconut milk
700g./1½lb. whiting fillets, skinned and cut into 2½cm./1in. pieces	1½ lb. whiting fillets, skinned and cut into 1in. pieces
300ml./10fl.oz. thick coconut milk	1¼ cups thick coconut milk

Heat the oil in a large frying-pan. When it is hot, add the garlic and shallots and fry, stirring occasionally, for 1 minute. Add the ginger and fry for a further 1 minute, stirring occasionally. Mix the lemon juice and water together, then pour into the pan. Reduce the heat to low, then stir in the lemon rind, chilli and turmeric. Bring to the boil.

Reduce the heat to low and pour in the thin coconut milk. When the milk is bubbling gently, add the fish pieces and thick coconut milk. Reduce the heat to low, cover the pan and simmer for 20 minutes, or until the fish is cooked through.

Transfer the mixture to a warmed serving bowl and serve at once.

Serves 4
Preparation and cooking time: 45 minutes

White Fish Curry

Metric/Imperial	American
3 Tbs. vegetable oil	3 Tbs. vegetable oil
2 medium onions, chopped	2 medium onions, chopped
4 garlic cloves, crushed	4 garlic cloves, crushed
2½cm./1in. piece of fresh root ginger, peeled and chopped	1in. piece of fresh green ginger, peeled and chopped
6 green chillis, chopped	6 green chillis, chopped
1 tsp. turmeric	1 tsp. turmeric
2 tsp. ground coriander	2 tsp. ground coriander
¼ tsp. black pepper	¼ tsp. black pepper
300ml./10fl.oz. thin coconut milk	1¼ cups thin coconut milk
1kg./2lb. cod steaks	2lb. cod steaks
450ml./15fl.oz. thick coconut milk	2 cups thick coconut milk
1 tsp. salt	1 tsp. salt
2 Tbs. lemon juice	2 Tbs. lemon juice
1 tsp. sugar	1 tsp. sugar
1 Tbs. chopped coriander leaves	1 Tbs. chopped coriander leaves

Heat the oil in a saucepan. When it is hot, add the onions and fry, stirring occasionally, until they are golden brown. Add the garlic, ginger and chillis and fry for 3 minutes, stirring frequently. Add the spices and pepper and fry for 2 minutes. Pour in the coconut milk and stir well. Add the fish, bring to the boil and cook for 5 minutes. Pour in the thick coconut milk and salt and reduce the heat to low.

Simmer for 20 minutes, or until the fish is cooked and flakes easily. Remove from the heat and stir in the lemon juice and sugar.

Transfer to a warmed serving dish and sprinkle over the coriander before serving.

Serves 6
Preparation and cooking time: 45 minutes

Machee Kabab

(Fish Kebabs)

Metric/Imperial	American
300ml./10fl.oz. yoghurt	1¼ cups yogurt
2 Tbs. flour	2 Tbs. flour
2 garlic cloves, crushed	2 garlic cloves, crushed
2 tsp. crushed coriander seeds	2 tsp. crushed coriander seeds
1 small dried chilli, crushed	1 small dried chilli, crushed
½ tsp. garam masala	½ tsp. garam masala
juice of 1 lemon	juice of 1 lemon
1kg./2lb. firm white fish fillets, cubed	2lb. firm white fish fillets, cubed

Combine all the ingredients, except the fish, in a large shallow bowl. Stir in the fish gently and set aside to marinate at room temperature for 30 minutes, basting occasionally.

Preheat the grill (broiler) to moderate. Thread the cubes on to skewers and reserve the marinade. Arrange the skewers in a lined grill (broiler) pan and grill (broil) for 10 to 12 minutes, turning occasionally and basting with the marinade, or until the cubes are cooked through.

Slide the cubes off the skewers on to a warmed serving dish and serve at once.

Serves 4-6
Preparation and cooking time: 50 minutes

Tandoori Machee

(Marinated Spiced Fish)

Metric/Imperial	American
4 large red mullets, or any similar oily fish, cleaned and gutted	4 large red mullets, or any similar oily fish, cleaned and gutted
juice of 2 lemons	juice of 2 lemons
75g./3oz. butter, melted	6 Tbs. butter, melted
2 tsp. ground cumin	2 tsp. ground cumin
1 lemon, thinly sliced	1 lemon, thinly sliced

MARINADE	MARINADE
50ml./2fl.oz. yogurt	¼ cup yogurt
2 garlic cloves, crushed	2 garlic cloves, crushed
4cm./1½in. piece of fresh root ginger, peeled and chopped	1½in. piece of fresh green ginger, peeled and chopped
1 Tbs. coriander seeds	1 Tbs. coriander seeds
1 tsp. garam masala	1 tsp. garam masala
2 dried red chillis	2 dried red chillis
red food colouring	red food coloring

Make slits along both sides of the fish, about 2½cm./1in. apart. Rub all over with the lemon juice and set aside for 10 minutes.

To make the marinade, combine all the ingredients, except the food colouring, in a blender and blend to a paste. Stir in the food colouring. Put the fish in a shallow bowl and spoon over the marinade, turning to coat the fish thoroughly. Set aside to marinate at room temperature for 6 hours, basting occasionally. Remove from the marinade and arrange the fish on individual skewers. Arrange the skewers on the rack of a roasting tin and put the tin into the oven. Bake for 10 minutes. Combine the melted butter and ground cumin together, then brush over the fish. Return to the oven and cook for a further 5 to 8 minutes, or until the fish is cooked and flakes easily.

Remove from the oven and slide the fish on to a warmed serving dish. Garnish with the lemon slices before serving.

Serves 4

Preparation and cooking time: 6¾ hours

Tali Machee

(Deep-Fried Spiced Fish)

Metric/Imperial	American
8 lemon sole fillets	8 lemon sole fillets
salt and pepper	salt and pepper
juice of 2 lemons	juice of 2 lemons
vegetable oil for deep-frying	vegetable oil for deep-frying
BATTER	BATTER
75g./3oz. besan or chick-pea flour	¾ cup besan or chick-pea flour
25g./1oz. rice flour	¼ cup rice flour
1 tsp. turmeric	1 tsp. turmeric
1 tsp. hot chilli powder	1 tsp. hot chilli powder
125ml./4fl.oz. water	½ cup water

Cut each fillet in half, then rub all over with salt and pepper. Transfer the pieces to a large bowl. Sprinkle over the lemon juice and set aside for 1 hour.

Meanwhile, prepare the batter. Combine all the ingredients, beating until they form a smooth batter the consistency of single (light) cream.

Remove the fish from the lemon juice and pat dry with kitchen towels. Dip each piece into the batter to coat it thoroughly.

Fill a large deep-frying pan one-third full with oil and heat it until it is hot. Carefully lower the fish pieces into the oil, a few at a time, and fry for 5 minutes, or until they are crisp and golden brown. Drain on kitchen towels and transfer to a warmed serving dish before serving.

Serves 4

Preparation and cooking time: 1½ hours

Tali Machee is a delicious, savoury dish comprising sole fillets coated in batter and deep-fried until golden brown.

ACCOMPANIMENTS

Basic Basmati Rice

Metric/Imperial	American
275g./10oz. basmati or other long-grain rice, soaked in cold water for 30 minutes and drained	1⅔ cups basmati or other long-grain rice, soaked in cold water for 30 minutes and drained
600ml./1 pint water	2½ cups water
1 tsp. salt	1 tsp. salt

Put the rice in a saucepan and pour over the water and salt. Bring to the boil, cover the pan and reduce the heat to low. Simmer for 15 to 20 minutes, or until the rice is cooked and the liquid is absorbed.

Remove from the heat and serve at once.

Serves 4

Preparation and cooking time: 1 hour

Kaha Buth

(Sri Lankan Yellow Rice)

Metric/Imperial	American
50g./2oz. ghee or clarified butter	4 Tbs. ghee or clarified butter
2 medium onions, chopped	2 medium onions, chopped
1 garlic clove, crushed	1 garlic clove, crushed
4 curry or bay leaves	4 curry or bay leaves
450g./1lb. long-grain rice, washed, soaked in cold water for 30 minutes and drained	2⅔ cups long-grain rice, washed, soaked in cold water for 30 minutes and drained
10 black peppercorns	10 black peppercorns
1 tsp. chopped lemon grass or grated lemon rind	1 tsp. chopped lemon grass or grated lemon rind
5 whole cloves	5 whole cloves
1 tsp. crushed cardamom seeds	1 tsp. crushed cardamom seeds
½ tsp. saffron threads, soaked in 2 Tbs. boiling water for 10 minutes	½ tsp. saffron threads, soaked in 2 Tbs. boiling water for 10 minutes
1¼l./2 pints coconut milk	5 cups coconut milk
GARNISH	GARNISH
1 Tbs. ghee or clarified butter	1 Tbs. ghee or clarified butter
1 tomato, sliced	1 tomato, sliced
4 Tbs. sultanas	4 Tbs. seedless raisins
2 Tbs. cashewnuts	2 Tbs. cashewnuts
1 hard-boiled egg, sliced	1 hard-boiled egg, sliced

Melt the ghee in a large saucepan. Add the onions, garlic and curry or bay leaves and fry, stirring occasionally, until the onions are soft. Add the rice and fry for 3 minutes, stirring frequently. Stir in the peppercorns, lemon grass or rind, cloves, cardamom seeds and saffron threads until the mixture is slightly yellow. Pour over the coconut milk and bring to the boil.

Reduce the heat to low, cover the pan and simmer the rice for 15 to 20 minutes, or until it is cooked and tender and the liquid absorbed.

Meanwhile, make the garnish. Melt the ghee in a small frying-pan. Add the tomato, sultanas (raisins) and cashews and fry gently for 2 to 3 minutes, or until they are just beginning to turn brown. Remove from the heat.

Remove the whole spices from the rice and transfer it to a warmed serving dish. Arrange the tomatoes, sultanas (raisins) cashewnuts and egg slices decoratively over the top and sides and serve at once.

Serves 6
Preparation and cooking time: 45 minutes

Saffron Rice

Metric/Imperial	American
50g./2oz. butter	4 Tbs. butter
2 tsp. cardamom seeds	2 tsp. cardamom seeds
4 cloves	4 cloves
3 cinnamon sticks	3 cinnamon sticks
1 medium onion, chopped	1 medium onion, chopped
350g./12oz. long-grain rice, soaked in cold water for 30 minutes and drained	2 cups long-grain rice, soaked in cold water for 30 minutes and drained
725ml./1¼ pints boiling chicken stock	3 cups boiling chicken stock
1 tsp. salt	1 tsp. salt
¾ tsp. crushed saffron threads, soaked in 2 Tbs. boiling water	¾ tsp. crushed saffron threads, soaked in 2 Tbs. boiling water

Melt the butter in a saucepan. Add the spices and fry for 2 minutes, stirring constantly. Add the onion and fry, stirring occasionally, until it is golden brown. Add the rice, reduce the heat to moderately low and simmer for 5 minutes, stirring constantly. Pour over the boiling stock, and stir in the salt and saffron mixture. Cover the pan, reduce the heat to low and simmer for 15 to 20 minutes, or until the rice is cooked and the water absorbed.

Remove from the heat and serve at once.

Serves 4-6
Preparation and cooking time: 1 hour

Cachoombar

(Onion Salad)

Metric/Imperial	American
2 medium onions, very finely chopped	2 medium onions, very finely chopped
2 large tomatoes, finely chopped	2 large tomatoes, finely chopped
½ medium cucumber, very finely chopped	½ medium cucumber, very finely chopped
2 green chillis, seeded and finely chopped	2 green chillis, seeded and finely chopped
1 Tbs. chopped coriander leaves	1 Tbs. chopped coriander leaves
75ml./3fl.oz. wine vinegar	6 Tbs. wine vinegar

Combine the onions, tomatoes, cucumber and chillis in a shallow bowl. Sprinkle over the coriander and vinegar and toss gently to coat. Cover and chill in the refrigerator for 20 minutes before serving.

Serves 3-4
Preparation time: 30 minutes

Vellarikai Pachadi

(Cucumber and Yogurt Salad)

Metric/Imperial	American
1 cucumber, peeled and finely chopped	1 cucumber, peeled and finely chopped
½ fresh coconut	½ fresh coconut
2 green chillis	2 green chillis
450ml./15fl.oz. yogurt	2 cups yogurt
1 tsp. salt	1 tsp. salt
2 tsp. vegetable oil	2 tsp. vegetable oil
1 tsp. mustard seeds	1 tsp. mustard seeds

Vellarikai Pachadi is a refreshing salad made with cucumber and yogurt and suitable for serving with most curries.

Put the cucumber into a colander and drain for 1 hour.

Pare the thin brown skin of the coconut and cut the flesh into pieces. Put the

coconut pieces and chillis into a blender with 2 to 3 tablespoons of water and blend to form a smooth purée. Transfer to a serving bowl and beat in the yogurt, cucumber and salt.

Heat the oil in a small frying-pan. When it is hot, add the mustard seeds. Cover and fry until they begin to spatter. Stir the seeds and oil into the yogurt. Cover and chill in the refrigerator for 1 hour.

Serve chilled.

Serves 4-6
Preparation and cooking time: 1 hour 10 minutes

Cucumber Raita

(Cucumber and Yogurt Salad)

Metric/Imperial	American
600ml./1 pint yogurt	2½ cups yogurt
½ cucumber, washed and diced	½ cucumber, washed and diced
4 spring onions, finely chopped	4 scallions, finely chopped
salt and pepper	salt and pepper
1 green chilli finely chopped	1 green chilli, finely chopped
¼ tsp. paprika	¼ tsp. paprika

Beat the yogurt until it is smooth, then beat in the cucumber, spring onions (scallions) and seasoning. Spoon into a serving bowl, cover and chill in the refrigerator for 1 hour.

Sprinkle over the chilli and paprika before serving.

Serves 4-6
Preparation time: 1 hour 10 minutes

Banana Raita

(Banana and Yogurt Salad)

Metric/Imperial	American
600ml./1 pint yogurt	2½ cups yogurt
4 bananas, sliced	4 bananas, sliced
2 green chillis, finely chopped	2 green chillis, finely chopped
1 Tbs. lemon juice	1 Tbs. lemon juice
1 tsp. garam masala	1 tsp. garam masala
¼ tsp. ground coriander	¼ tsp. ground coriander
½ tsp. salt	½ tsp. salt
2 tsp. chopped coriander leaves	2 tsp. chopped coriander leaves

Beat the yogurt until it is smooth, then beat in the bananas, chillis, lemon juice, spices and salt. Spoon into a serving bowl, cover and chill for 1 hour.

Sprinkle over the coriander before serving.

Serves 4-6
Preparation time: 1 hour 10 minutes

Guava Raita

(Guava and Yogurt Salad)

Metric/Imperial	American
600ml./1 pint yogurt	2½ cups yogurt
2 canned guavas, drained and diced	2 canned guavas, drained and diced
½ tsp. salt	½ tsp. salt
1 Tbs. ghee or clarified butter	1 Tbs. ghee or clarified butter
1 tsp. mustard seeds	1 tsp. mustard seeds
1 green chilli, finely chopped	1 green chilli, finely chopped
2 tsp. coriander leaves	2 tsp. chopped coriander leaves

Beat the yogurt until it is smooth, then beat in the cucumber, guavas and salt.
Melt the ghee or clarified butter in a small frying-pan. Add the mustard seeds,
cover and cook until the seeds begin to spatter. Add the chilli and fry for 10
seconds, stirring constantly. Stir the contents of the pan into the yogurt mixture.
Spoon into a serving bowl, cover and chill in the refrigerator for 1 hour.

Shrimp Sambal is a fiery side dish made with shrimps and is generally served with vegetable or fish curries.

   Sprinkle over the coriander before serving.

Serves 4-6

Preparation and cooking time: 1 hour 10 minutes

Pol Sambola 1

Metric/Imperial	American
2 medium tomatoes, blanched, peeled and chopped	2 medium tomatoes, blanched, peeled and chopped
2 small onions, finely chopped	2 small onions, finely chopped
1 green chilli, finely chopped	1 green chilli, finely chopped
2 Tbs. lime or lemon juice	2 Tbs. lime or lemon juice
2 Tbs. desiccated coconut	2 Tbs. shredded coconut

Combine the tomatoes, onions and chilli, then pour over the lime or lemon juice. Spoon the mixture into a shallow serving bowl. Sprinkle over the coconut, cover and chill in the refrigerator until ready to serve.

Serves 3-4
Preparation and cooking tiem: 10 minutes

Pol Sambola 11

In Sri Lanka, Maldive fish, a dried tuna delicacy, is added to this sambal – if you wish to be authentic and add it or an equivalent (and if Maldive fish is unavailable) dried prawns (available from Chinese stores) or Japanese katsuobushi (dried bonito fish) can be substituted. For convenience, however, it is omitted from the recipe as given below.

Metric/Imperial	American
125g./4oz. desiccated coconut	1 cup shredded coconut
$\frac{1}{2}$ tsp. hot chilli powder	$\frac{1}{2}$ tsp. hot chilli powder
1 tsp. paprika	1 tsp. paprika
$\frac{1}{4}$ tsp. finely chopped lemon grass or finely grated lemon rind	$\frac{1}{4}$ tsp. finely chopped lemon grass or finely grated lemon rind
1 Tbs. lemon juice	1 Tbs. lemon juice
3 Tbs. grated onion	3 Tbs. grated onion
3 Tbs. coconut milk	3 Tbs. coconut milk

Combine the coconut, chilli powder, paprika and lemon rind in a small serving bowl. Gradually stir in the lemon juice, grated onion and coconut milk until the mixture is moistened.

Serve at once.

Serves 4
Preparation time: 5 minutes

Shrimp Sambal

Metric/Imperial	American
175g./6oz. cooked shrimps, chopped	6oz. cooked shrimps, chopped
2 hard-boiled eggs, sliced	2 hard-boiled eggs, sliced
1 medium onion, finely chopped	1 medium onion, finely chopped

1 green chilli, chopped	1 green chilli, chopped
2½cm./1in. piece of fresh root ginger, peeled and chopped	1in. piece of fresh green ginger, peeled and chopped
½ tsp. hot chilli powder	½ tsp. hot chilli powder
2 Tbs. thick coconut milk	2 Tbs. thick coconut milk
¼ tsp. cumin seeds, coarsely crushed	¼ tsp. cumin seeds, coarsely crushed

Combine all the ingredients except the cumin seeds, then spoon the mixture into a shallow serving bowl. Sprinkle over the cumin, cover and chill in the refrigerator until ready to serve.
Serves 3-4
Preparation time: 10 minutes

Pipinge Sambal

(Cucumber Sambal)

Metric/Imperial	American
1 large cucumber	1 large cucumber
1½ Tbs. salt	1½ Tbs. salt
2 spring onions, very finely chopped	2 scallions, very finely chopped
2 red chillis, very finely chopped	2 red chillis, very finely chopped
½ tsp. turmeric	½ tsp. turmeric
1 Tbs. lemon juice	1 Tbs. lemon juice
125ml./4fl.oz. very thick coconut milk	½ cup very thick coconut milk

Peel the cucumber, then chop into small dice. Transfer to a colander and sprinkle liberally with the salt. Set aside at room temperature for 30 minutes. Rinse the cucumber under cold running water, then pat dry with kitchen towels.

Transfer the cucumber to a medium serving bowl. Gradually add all the remaining ingredients until the mixture is thoroughly blended.

Chill in the refrigerator until ready to use.
Serves 4-6
Preparation time: 35 minutes

BREAD

Chapatti

(Unleavened Bread)

Metric/Imperial	American
225g./8oz. wholewheat flour	2 cups wholemeal flour
salt	salt
50g./2oz. butter	4 Tbs. butter
150ml./5fl.oz. water	$\frac{2}{3}$ cup water
1 Tbs. ghee or clarified butter	1 Tbs. ghee or clarified butter

Sift the flour and a little salt into a large bowl. Add the butter and rub into the flour. Make a well in the centre and pour in 75ml./3fl.oz. ($\frac{1}{3}$ cup) of water. Gradually add the rest of the water, mixing it in with your fingers. Form the dough into a ball and transfer to a floured board. Knead for about 10 minutes, or until elastic. Put the dough in a bowl, cover and set aside at room temperature for 30 minutes.

Divide the dough into eight portions. Roll out each portion into a thin, round shape, about 15cm./6in. in diameter.

Meanwhile, heat a heavy frying-pan over moderate heat. When it is hot, put one dough shape into the pan. When small blisters appear on the surface, press to flatten the dough. Turn over and cook until it is pale golden. Remove from the pan and brush with a little ghee or clarified butter. Arrange on a plate and cook the other chapattis in the same way.

Serve warm.

Serves 8
Preparation and cooking time: 55 minutes

Chapatti, the staple cereal food of Northern India, is one of the most common accompaniments to Indian meals.

Puris are deep-fried whole meal (wholewheat) breads and are delicious served with dry Indian vegetable or meat dishes.

Puris

(Deep-Fried Wholemeal Bread)

Metric/Imperial	American
225g./8oz. wholewheat flour	2 cups wholemeal flour
salt	salt
1 Tbs. butter	1 Tbs. butter
50ml./2fl.oz. tepid water	¼ cup tepid water
vegetable oil for deep-frying	vegetable oil for deep-frying

Combine the flour and a little salt in a bowl. Add the ghee or clarified butter and rub into the flour until it is absorbed. Add the water and mix and knead the ingredients to make a firm dough.

Turn the dough out on to a floured surface and knead for about 10 minutes, or until elastic. Pat into a ball and return to the bowl. Cover and set aside at room temperature for 30 minutes.

Remove the dough from the bowl. Pinch off small pieces of the dough and shape into balls. Flatten the balls and roll them out into circles, about 12cm./5in. in diameter.

Fill a large deep-frying pan one-third full with oil and heat until it is hot. Drop the pieces, one at a time, into the oil. Using a spatula or fish slice, press down and fry for 1 minute. Turn over and press down again. Fry for 30 seconds or until the puri is puffed up and golden.

Remove the puri from the pan and keep warm while you cook the remaining puris in the same way. Serve hot or warm.

Makes about 12
Preparation and cooking time: 1½ hours

Paratha

(Fried Wholemeal Bread)

Metric/Imperial	American
225g./8oz. wholewheat flour	2 cups wholemeal flour
salt	salt
125g./4oz. ghee or clarified butter, melted	8 Tbs. ghee of clarified butter, melted
50-125ml./2-4fl.oz. water	¼-½ cup water

Combine the flour and a little salt in a bowl. Add about a quarter of the ghee or clarified butter and rub into the flour until it is absorbed. Pour in 50ml./2fl.oz. (¼ cup) of the water and knead until the mixture forms a soft dough. If it is too dry mix in the remaining water, a little at a time, until the dough is soft and comes away from the sides of the bowl.

Turn the dough out on to a floured surface and knead for about 10 minutes, or until elastic. Pat into a ball and return to the bowl. Cover and set aside at room temperature for 1 hour.

Remove the dough from the bowl and knead lightly. Divide into four equal portions and shape each portion into a ball. Roll out into a thin circle. Brush each circle with a little of the remaining ghee or clarified butter. Fold the circles in half, then into quarters. Roll out into circles again, brush again with ghee or clarified butter and repeat the process again until all but 2 tablespoons of the ghee or clarified butter has been used up. Roll out each dough portion into a circle, about 18cm./7in. in diameter.

Lightly grease a heavy frying-pan with a little of the remaining ghee or clarified butter. When it is hot, add a paratha and cook, moving with your fingers occasionally, for 3 to 4 minutes, or until the underside is lightly browned. Brush the top with a little of the remaining ghee or clarified butter and, using your fingers, turn over and continue cooking for a further 3 minutes, or until the paratha is browned all over.

Remove from the pan and keep warm while you cook the remaining parathas in the same way. Serve hot.

Makes 4
Preparation and cooking time: 2 hours

CHUTNEY

Mango Chutney

Metric/Imperial	American
1½kg./3lb. mangoes, peeled, halved and stoned	3lb. mangoes, peeled, halved and pitted
75g./3oz. salt	¾ cup salt
450g./1lb. sugar	2 cups sugar
600ml./1 pint white wine vinegar	2½ cups white wine vinegar
5cm./2in. piece of fresh root ginger, peeled and chopped	2in. piece of fresh green ginger, peeled and chopped
6 garlic cloves, crushed	6 garlic cloves, crushed
2 tsp. hot chilli powder	2 tsp. hot chilli powder
1 cinnamon stick	1 cinnamon stick
125g./4oz. stoned dates	⅔ cup pitted dates
125g./4oz. raisins	⅔ cup raisins

Chop the mangoes finely and put in a bowl. Add the salt and about 2l./3½ pints (8¾ cups) of water. Cover and set aside for 24 hours.

Put the sugar and vinegar into a saucepan and bring to the boil. stirring until the sugar has dissolved. Stir in the mangoes, then add all the remaining ingredients and bring to the boil, stirring occasionally. Reduce the heat to low and simmer for about 1½ hours, stirring occasionally, or until the chutney is very thick.

Remove the cinnamon stick and ladel the chutney into warmed, sterilized jars. Cover, label and set aside until ready to use.

Makes about two 1kg./2lb. jars
Preparation and cooking time: 25½ hours

Date Chutney

Metric/Imperial	American
450g./1lb. canned peeled tomatoes	1lb. canned peeled tomatoes
225g./8oz. stoned dates, chopped	1⅓ cups pitted dates, chopped
125g./4oz. raisins	⅔ cup raisins
125g./4oz. currants	⅔ cup currants
125ml./4fl.oz. vinegar	½ cup vinegar
1 tsp. salt	1 tsp. salt
1 tsp. cayenne pepper	1 tsp. cayenne pepper

Put all the ingredients into a saucepan and bring slowly to the boil, stirring occasionally. Reduce the heat to very low and simmer for 1 to 1½ hours, stirring occasionally, or until it is very thick.

Ladle the chutney into warmed, sterilized jars. Cover, label and set aside until ready to use.

Makes about 1kg./2lb.
Preparation and cooking time: 1¾ hours

(1) Chillis sold whole or ground.
(2) Peppercorns – buy fresh and grind only when required.
(3) Turmeric available in sticks or as ground seeds.
(4) Cardamom sold as pods or as ground seeds.
(5) Paprika – ground seeds of the red pepper.
(6) A mineral – Salt found in coarse or fine form.
(7) Cumin seeds – heat before use for flavour.
(8) Coriander leaves used as a garnish; its seeds sold whole or ground.
(9) Saffron available whole, in threads, or ground.
(10) Nutmeg sold whole or ground.
(11) Ginger found fresh (green), crystallized or dried.
(12) Green chillis (see 1)
(13) Garlic sold in bulbs.
(14) Mace, outer shell of Nutmeg, available as blades or in powdered form.
(15) Turmeric (see 3)
(16) Red chillis (see 1)
(17) Red chillis (see 1)
(18) Cinnamon sold in bark form as sticks or as powder.
(19) Coriander (see 8)

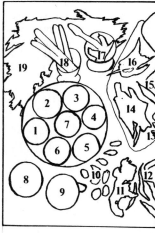

Lemon & Mustard Seed Chutney

Metric/Imperial	American
3 lemons, chopped and seeds removed	3 lemons, chopped and seeds removed
1 Tbs. salt	1 Tbs. salt
3 small onions, finely chopped	3 small onions, finely chopped
300ml./10fl.oz. vinegar	1¼ cups vinegar
1 tsp. garam masala	1 tsp. garam masala
2 Tbs. mustard seeds	2 Tbs. mustard seeds
225g./8oz. sugar	1 cup sugar
50g./2oz. raisins	⅓ cup raisins

Put the lemons into a bowl and sprinkle with salt. Cover and set aside for 10 hours.

Transfer the salted lemons to a saucepan and add all the remaining ingredients. Bring to the boil, reduce the heat to low, cover and simmer for 1 hour, or until the lemons are very soft.

Ladle the chutney into warmed, sterilized jars. Cover, label and set aside until ready to use.

Makes about 1kg./2lb.

Preparation and cooking time: 1½ hours

Tamatar Chatni

Metric/Imperial	American
1kg./2lb. tomatoes, blanched, peeled and chopped	2lb. tomatoes, blanched, peeled and chopped
450ml./15fl.oz. white vinegar	2 cups white vinegar
2 onions, finely chopped	2 onions, finely chopped
1 Tbs. salt	1 Tbs. salt
350g./12oz. soft brown sugar	2 cups soft brown sugar
4cm./1½in. piece of fresh root ginger, peeled and chopped	1½in. piece of fresh green ginger, peeled and chopped
3 garlic cloves, finely chopped	3 garlic cloves, finely chopped
3 dried red chillis, finely chopped	3 dried red chillis, finely chopped
10 cloves	10 cloves
2 cinnamon sticks	2 cinnamon sticks
½ tsp. crushed cardamom seeds	½ tsp. crushed cardamom seeds
50ml./2fl.oz. vegetable oil	¼ cup vegetable oil
1 Tbs. mustard seeds	1 Tbs. mustard seeds

Combine all the ingredients, except the oil and mustard seeds, in a saucepan and bring slowly to the boil, stirring occasionally. Reduce the heat to low and simmer for 5 hours, stirring occasionally, or until the mixture is very thick.

Meanwhile, heat the oil in a small frying-pan. When it is hot, add the mustard seeds and cover. When they stop spattering, turn the mixture into the pan with the other ingredients, stirring constantly. Simmer for a further 15 minutes.

Ladle the chutney into warmed, sterilized jars. Cover, label and set aside until ready to use.

Banana and Raisin Chutney

Metric/Imperial	American
1½kg./3lb. bananas, chopped	3lb. bananas, chopped
700g./1½lb. onions, chopped	1½lb. onions, chopped
2 large garlic cloves, crushed	2 large garlic cloves, crushed
1 tsp. salt	1 tsp. salt
juice and grated rind of 1 orange	juice and grated rind of 1 orange
450g./1lb. raisins	2⅔ cups raisins
2 Tbs. ground cumin	2 Tbs. ground cumin
2 Tbs. ground cardamom	2 Tbs. ground cardamom
2 Tbs. ground coriander	2 Tbs. ground coriander
1 tsp. cayenne pepper	1 tsp. cayenne pepper
600ml./1 pint white wine vinegar	2½ cups white wine vinegar

Put all the ingredients into a saucepan and bring slowly to the boil, stirring occasionally. Reduce the heat to very low and simmer for 1¼ hours, stirring occasionally.

Ladle the chutney into warmed, sterilized jars. Cover, label and set aside until ready for use.

Makes five ½kg./1lb. jars
Preparation and cooking time: 1½ hours

Nariel Chatni

Metric/Imperial	American
50g./2oz. desiccated coconut, soaked in 150ml./5fl.oz. yogurt for 1 hour	½ cup shredded coconut, soaked in ⅔ cup yogurt for 1 hour
juice and grated rind of 1 lemon	juice and grated rind of 1 lemon
2½cm./1in. piece of fresh root ginger, peeled and chopped	1in. piece of fresh root ginger, peeled and chopped
1 green chilli, chopped	1 green chilli, chopped
1 garlic clove, chopped	1 garlic clove, chopped
1 medium onion, chopped	1 medium onion, chopped

Put the coconut mixture and lemon juice in a blender and blend to a smooth purée. Stir in the remaining ingredients and blend for 1 minute more.

Spoon into a small serving bowl and chill in the refrigerator until ready to serve.

Makes about 125g./4oz. (1 cup)
Preparation time: 10 minutes

Apricot, Carrot and Swede (Rutabaga) Chutney

Metric/Imperial	American
450g./1lb. dried apricots	2⅔ cups dried apricots
900ml./1½ pints distilled malt vinegar	3¾ cups distilled malt vinegar
½kg./1lb. swedes, peeled and chopped	1lb. rutabagas, peeled and chopped
½kg./1lb. carrots, chopped	1lb. carrots, chopped
½kg./1lb. onions, chopped	1lb. onions, chopped
225g./8oz. Demerara sugar	1⅓ cups light brown sugar
2 tsp. ground mace	2 tsp. ground mace
2 tsp. cayenne pepper	2 tsp. cayenne pepper

Put the apricots in a bowl and pour over 600ml./1 pint (2½ cups) of the vinegar. Set aside to soak overnight. Drain, reserve the vinegar and chop the apricots finely. Put all the ingredients into a saucepan and bring slowly to the boil. Reduce the heat to very low and simmer for 1 hour, stirring occasionally.

Ladle the chutney into warmed, sterilized jars. Cover, label and set aside until ready to use.

Makes five ½kg./1lb. jars
Preparation and cooking time: 14 hours

Adrak Chatni

(Ginger Chutney)

This chutney does not keep well and should be eaten within two days of making.

Metric/Imperial	American
juice of 2 lemons	juice of 2 lemons
4 tsp. sugar	4 tsp. sugar
125g./4oz fresh root ginger, peeled and chopped	4oz. fresh green ginger, peeled and chopped
75g./3oz. sultanas	½ cup seedless raisins
1 garlic clove	1 garlic clove
1½ tsp. salt	1½ tsp. salt

Put the juice of 1½ lemons, 2 teaspoons of sugar and all the other ingredients into a blender and blend to a smooth purée. Add the remaining lemon juice and the sugar and stir well.

Spoon into a small serving bowl and chill in the refrigerator until ready to serve.

Serves 6
Preparation time: 10 minutes

Date and Banana Chutney

Metric/Imperial	American
6 bananas, sliced	6 bananas, sliced
4 medium onions, chopped	4 medium onions, chopped
225g./8oz. stoned dates, chopped	1⅓ cups chopped pitted dates
300ml./10fl.oz. vinegar	1¼ cups vinegar
1 tsp. curry powder	1 tsp. curry powder
125g./4oz. crystallized ginger, chopped	⅔ cup chopped candied ginger
½ tsp. salt	½ tsp. salt
250ml./8fl.oz. dark treacle	1 cup molasses

Put the bananas, onions, dates and vinegar into a saucepan and cook for about 15 minutes, or until the onions are tender. Remove from the heat and mash the mixture to a pulp, or purée the mixture in a blender. Stir in the curry powder, ginger, salt and treacle (molasses).

Return the ingredients to the saucepan and return the pan to moderate heat. Cook for 15 to 20 minutes, stirring occasionally, or until the mixture is a rich brown colour.

Remove from the heat and ladle the chutney into warmed, sterilized jars. Cover, label and set aside until ready to use.

Makes about 1½kg./1 lb.
Preparation and cooking time: 1 hour

Chutneys are ideal to serve as accompaniments to Indian meals as they add variety of flavour, texture and taste.

Tamarind Sauce

Metric/Imperial	American
225g./8oz. tamarind	1 cup tamarind
900ml./1½ pints boiling water	3¾ cups boiling water
1 tsp. salt	1 tsp. salt
4cm./1½in. piece of fresh root ginger, peeled and chopped	1½in. piece of fresh green ginger, peeled and chopped
2 Tbs. jaggery or raw sugar	2 Tbs. jaggery or raw sugar
½ tsp. hot chilli powder	½ tsp. hot chilli powder

Put the tamarind into a bowl and pour over the boiling water. Set aside for 1 hour. Break up the pulp slightly with your fingers, then push through a fine strainer held over a small saucepan, rubbing as much of the pulp through as possible with the back of a wooden spoon. Discard the contents of the strainer.

Place the pan over moderate heat and stir in the remaining ingredients. Reduce the heat to low and simmer for 20 minutes, stirring occasionally.

Pour into a warmed sauceboat and set aside to cool slightly before serving.
Makes about 425ml./14fl.oz. (1¾ cups)
Preparation and cooking time: 1½ hours

Lime Pickle

Metric/Imperial	American
10 limes	10 limes
10 green chillis	10 green chillis
3 Tbs. coarse rock salt	3 Tbs. coarse rock salt
2 bay leaves, crumbled	2 bay leaves, crumbled
75g./3oz. fresh root ginger, peeled and cut into strips	3oz. fresh green ginger, peeled and cut into strips
300ml./10fl.oz. lime juice	1¼ cups lime juice

Wash the limes and dry on kitchen towels. Using a stainless steel knife, make four cuts through the limes to quarter them to within ½cm./¼in. of the bottom. Remove the pips (stones). Slit the chillis, lengthways, and scrape out the seeds, leaving the chillis whole with the stalks.

Arrange a layer of limes on the bottom of a pickling jar. Sprinkle with salt and bay leaves, then add 1 to 2 chillis and about 1 tablespoon of ginger. Repeat these layers until all the ingredients, except half the salt, are used up. Pour in the lime juice and give the jar a good shake to settle the contents. Cover the mouth of the jar with a clean cloth and tie down with string. Put the jar in a sunny place for at least 6 days, adding half a tablespoon of the remaining salt each day. Shake the jar at least twice a day. Each night place the jar in a dry place in the kitchen. Be sure to turn the jar each day so that all sides are exposed to the sun's rays.

After all this, keep the pickle on a kitchen shelf for 10 days. Cover with a lid and shake the jar every day. After 10 days the pickle is ready to eat.
Makes about 900g./1½ lbs
Preparation time: 16 days

SWEETS

Nariel Samosas

(Coconut Turnovers)

Metric/Imperial	American
50g./2oz. desiccated coconut, soaked in 75ml./3fl.oz. milk	½ cup shredded coconut, soaked in ⅓ cup milk
½ tsp. crushed cardamom seeds	½ tsp. crushed cardamom seeds
50g./2oz. sultanas	⅓ cup seedless raisins
50g./2oz. soft brown sugar	⅓ cup soft brown sugar
1 egg white, lightly beaten	1 egg white, lightly beaten
350g./12oz. frozen puff pastry, thawed	12oz. frozen puff pastry, thawed

Preheat the oven to hot 220°C (Gas Mark 7, 425°F).

To make the filling, combine the coconut, cardamom and sultanas (raisins) and stir to mix.

Roll out the dough on a lightly floured surface and, using a 7½cm./3in. pastry cutter, cut the dough into about 24 thin circles. Put a spoonful of the coconut mixture in the centre of each circle and dampen the edges with water. Fold the dough over and crimp to seal.

Transfer the turnovers to a lightly greased baking sheet and brush with a little egg white. Bake for 15 to 20 minutes, or until the turnovers are crisp and golden brown.

Transfer to a wire rack to cool and serve slightly warm.
Makes 24
Preparation and cooking time: 45 minutes to 1 hour

Halva

(Semolina Dessert)

Metric/Imperial	American
350g./14oz. sugar	1¾ cups sugar
900ml./1½ pints water	3¾ cups water
2 tsp. cardamom seeds	2 tsp. cardamom seeds
3 cinnamon sticks	3 cinnamon sticks
225g./8oz. butter	1 cup butter
225g./8oz. semolina	2 cups semolina
125g./4oz. sultanas	⅔ cup seedless raisins
125g./4oz. slivered almonds	⅔ cup slivered almonds

Put the sugar and water into a large saucepan and put over high heat. Bring to the boil, stirring constantly until the sugar has dissolved. Stir in the cardamom and cinnamon. Remove from the heat.

Melt the butter in a saucepan. Stir in the semolina and reduce the heat to low. Simmer for 20 minutes, then stir in the remaining ingredients and the sugar syrup. Boil for 5 minutes, stirring constantly. Discard the cardamom and cinnamon.

Turn the mixture into a greased shallow dish or pan and set aside to cool. When the fudge is completely cool, cut into bars or other serving shapes.
Makes about 350g./10oz.
Preparation and cooking time: 2 hours

Rava Kheer

(Semolina and Milk Dessert)

Metric/Imperial	American
900ml./1½ pints milk	3¾ cups milk
2 Tbs. semolina	2 Tbs. semolina
2 Tbs. sugar	2 Tbs. sugar
1 Tbs. melted butter	1 Tbs. melted butter
1 Tbs. crushed cardamom seeds	1 Tbs. crushed cardamom seeds
½ tsp. grated nutmeg	½ tsp. grated nutmeg
1 tsp. rose water	1 tsp. rose water
2 Tbs. toasted flaked almonds	2 Tbs. toasted slivered almonds

Put the milk and semolina into a saucepan and bring to the boil, stirring constantly. Reduce the heat to low and simmer for 5 to 7 minutes, stirring constantly, or until the mixture is thick. Stir in the sugar and cook for 5 minutes, stirring constantly until the sugar has dissolved. Stir in the butter. Remove from the heat and stir in the cardamom, nutmeg and rose water.

Spoon into a greased shallow dish or pan and set aside to cool completely. Sprinkle over the almonds before serving.
Serves 6
Preparation and cooking time: 1¼ hours

Barfi

(Milk and Coconut Fudge)

Metric/Imperial	American
1 tsp. butter, softened	1 tsp. butter, softened
1¼l./2 pints milk	5 cups milk
125g./4oz. desiccated coconut	1 cup shredded coconut
125g./4oz. sugar	½ cup sugar
¼ tsp. carmine food colouring	¼ tsp. carmine food coloring
1 tsp. crushed cardamom seeds	1 tsp. crushed cardamom seeds

Bring the milk to the boil very slowly in a large, heavy saucepan. When it is bubbling, increase the heat and boil briskly, stirring constantly, for about 40 minutes, or until the milk is reduced by about half. Stir in the coconut and sugar, reduce the heat to low and cook for 10 minutes, stirring constantly, or until the mixture is very thick. Stir in the remaining ingredients.

Turn the mixture into a greased shallow dish or pan and set aside to cool. When the fudge is completely cool, cut into bars or other serving shapes.
Makes 350g./12oz.
Preparation and cooking time: 2 hours

Shrikhand

(Curd with Sugar and Saffron)

Metric/Imperial	American
2¼l./4 pints yogurt	5 pints yogurt
castor sugar	superfine sugar
½ tsp. ground saffron	½ tsp. ground saffron
1 Tbs. rose water	1 Tbs. rose water
2 Tbs. crushed cardamom seeds	2 Tbs. crushed cardamom seeds
15 pistachio nuts, blanched and sliced	15 pistachio nuts, blanched and sliced

Put the yogurt in a cheesecloth bag and tie over a mixing bowl. Drain for 2 hours, or until the whey has drained out. Discard the whey.

Weigh the curd left in the bag and transfer to a large bowl. For every 225g./8oz. (1 cup) of curd, stir in 175g./6oz. (¾ cup) of sugar. Stir in the remaining ingredients, reserving a few nuts for garnish. The mixture should have the consistency of thick cream.

Cover the bowl and chill in the refrigerator for 1 hour. Spoon into individual bowls, and sprinkle over the reserved nuts before serving.
Serves 8-10
Preparation time: 3¼ hours

Kulfi

(Ice-Cream)

Metric/Imperial	American
450ml./15fl.oz. mango juice	2 cups mango juice
150ml./5fl.oz. single cream	⅔ cup light cream
2 Tbs. castor sugar	2 Tbs. superfine sugar

Combine all the ingredients, then spoon into six small moulds. Tightly cover and freeze, shaking the moulds about three times during the first hour of freezing.

To serve, dip the bottoms of the moulds into boiling water for 2 seconds, then invert giving the moulds a sharp shake. The ice-cream should slide out easily. Serve at once.
Serves 6
Preparation time: 3 hours

BASIC RECIPES

Ghee

(Clarified Butter)

Metric/Imperial	American
450g./1lb. butter	2 cups butter

Put the butter into a heavy-based saucepan and melt very slowly over low heat. Be careful not to let the butter burn. Heat to just below boiling point, then simmer for 30 minutes, or until the moisture in the butter evaporates and the protein sinks to the bottom of the pan. Remove from the heat and carefully strain the clear fat through several thicknesses of cheesecloth into a jar.

Cover tightly and store in a cool, dry place. It will solidify as it cools.
Makes 350g./12oz. (1½ cups)
Preparation and cooking time: 45 minutes

Coconut Milk

Coconut milk is an important ingredient in many Indian recipes and this is a substitute if you cannot obtain fresh coconut milk. This recipe will produce a medium milk – add a little more creamed coconut for thick, and a little less for thin.

Metric/Imperial	American
7½cm./3in. slice creamed coconut	3in. slice creamed coconut
450ml./15fl.oz. boiling water	2 cups boiling water

Combine the ingredients together, stirring constantly until the coconut dissolves.
Makes about 500ml./18fl.oz. (2¼ cups)
Preparation time: 5 minutes

Home-Made Yogurt

Metric/Imperial	American
725-900ml./1¼-1½ pints milk	3-3¼ cups milk
2 Tbs. yogurt or yogurt culture	2 Tbs. yogurt or yogurt culture

Pour the milk into a saucepan and bring to the boil. Remove from the heat and allow to cool to 43°C (110°F) on a sugar thermometer, or until you can immerse a finger for 10 seconds without discomfort.

Meanwhile, beat the yogurt or yogurt culture in a glass or earthenware bowl to smooth. Add 3 tablespoons of the warmed milk, a little at a time, beating constantly until the mixture is blended. Beat in the remaining milk until the mixture is thoroughly blended. Cover, wrap in a towel and keep in a warm, draught-free place for 8 hours, or until it has thickened.

Store in the refrigerator until you are ready to use.

Makes 1¼l./2 pints (5 cups)
Preparation time: 8¼ hours

Garam Masala

(Mixed Ground Spices)
Garam masala can be bought commercially but in India it is often made at home. There are many versions -- this is a basic one.

Metric/Imperial	American
3 Tbs. black peppercorns, ground	3 Tbs. black peppercorns, ground
1 Tbs. ground cumin	1 Tbs. ground cumin
1 tsp. ground cinnamon	1 tsp. ground cinnamon
2 tsp. ground cardamom	2 tsp. ground cardamom
3 Tbs. ground coriander	3 Tbs. ground coriander
1 tsp. ground cloves	1 tsp. ground cloves
1½ tsp. ground mace	1½ tsp. ground mace
½ tsp. grated nutmeg	½ tsp. grated nutmeg

Combine all the ingredients together and store, covered, in a cool, dry place.
Makes about 50g./2oz. (½ cup)
Preparation time: 2 minutes

Curry Powder 1

Curry powder as it is known in the west is merely a dry 'masala' or concoction of mixed ground spices. Most recipes in this book conform to the standard Indian practice of adding several spices to any given dish, but you can prepare your own powder which can be used for basic meat or fish curries. If you use root ginger in the recipe, omit the ground ginger below.

Metric/Imperial	American
1 Tbs. ground coriander	1 Tbs. ground coriander
1 tsp. ground cumin	1 tsp. ground cumin
1 tsp. turmeric	1 tsp. turmeric
½ tsp. ground ginger	½ tsp. ground ginger
½ tsp. hot chilli powder	½ tsp. hot chilli powder

Combine all the ingredients in a small bowl. Add to the recipe in appropriate amounts.

Makes about 25g./1oz. ($\frac{1}{4}$ cup)
Preparation time: 2 minutes

Curry Powder II

This is a slightly sweeter, milder version and could be used for fish or shellfish, or vegetable dishes.

Metric/Imperial	American
1 Tbs. ground coriander	1 Tbs. ground coriander
$\frac{1}{2}$ tsp. ground cumin	$\frac{1}{2}$ tsp. ground cumin
1 tsp. turmeric	1 tsp. turmeric
$\frac{1}{2}$ tsp. garam masala	$\frac{1}{2}$ tsp. garam masala
$\frac{1}{4}$ tsp. ground fenugreek	$\frac{1}{4}$ tsp. ground fenugreek
$\frac{1}{4}$ tsp. ground cardamom	$\frac{1}{4}$ tsp. ground cardamom
$\frac{1}{4}$ tsp. hot chilli powder	$\frac{1}{4}$ tsp. hot chilli powder

Combine all the ingredients in a small bowl. Add to the recipe in appropriate amounts.

Makes about 15g./$\frac{1}{2}$oz. (2 tablespoons)
Preparation time: 2 minutes

GLOSSARY

Asafoetida
A dried gum resin, sometimes used as a spice in Indian cooking. It can be one of the spices used to make up the western 'curry' powder. Not easily obtainable in the West, although many oriental stores stock it. If unobtainable, omit from the recipe – there is no substitute.

Besan or Chick-pea flour
(Sometimes known as gram) used extensively in India, especially for batters for deep-frying. Oriental or Indian stores are the most likely stockists. If unobtainable, you *could* grind chick-peas in a blender, then sift to refine them sufficiently, or substitute ordinary flour or cornflour (cornstarch).

Cardamom
A spice widely used in Indian and Sri Lankan cooking. A member of the ginger family and one of the most expensive spices in the world. Used in both seed and ground form – the outer pods are usually discarded and the seeds bruised and added to recipes whole, or the seeds are ground to a powder. Obtainable from oriental stores and also from any good Scandinavian store.

Chilli
Used in Indian cooking either fresh or dried, to add 'heat' to recipes. Obtainable from oriental or Mexican stores. The seeds are the hottest part of the chilli, so if you wish to reduce the firiness of a dish, remove them and add only the chopped outer part. If fresh or dried chillis are difficult to obtain, substitute dried chilli powder – but make sure it is hot chilli powder and not the much milder chilli seasoning. About ½ teaspoon ground chilli is a rough equivalent of one chopped chilli.

Coconut milk
Used as a cooking stock all over India. If fresh coconut is not available a good substitute can be made from creamed coconut (see recipes). If creamed coconut is unavailable, then use desiccated (shredded) coconut instead. Put about 125g./4oz. of desiccated (shredded) coconut into a blender and pour over 300ml./10fl.oz./1¼ cups of boiling water. Soak for 10 minutes, then blend the mixture and strain through cheesecloth into a jug or bowl.

Coriander
Used in many ways in Indian cooking: as a ground spice, one of the necessary ingredients in a 'curry' sauce; as a seed used in many savoury recipes and as chopped leaves used as a garnish on almost everything. It is a member of the parsley family and if coriander leaves are unobtainable, fresh chopped parsley can be substituted. Ground and seeded coriander are available from most supermarkets. Coriander leaves can be bought from oriental, Greek or Mexican stores.

Curry leaves
Used fresh in India as either a garnish to curries, or as an ingredient to be added towards the end of cooking. Can be obtained dried from Indian provision stores. If unobtainable, either omit from the recipe or substitute bay leaves.

Dhal
The collective word for legumes or pulses. Lentils are the most popular form of dhal, and there are many varieties and colours found in India. In the sourthen part of the country, where many people are vegetarian, it forms an important part of the diet. If you cannot obtain the Indian varieties of lentil mentioned in the recipes, substitute the orange lentils widely available in the West. In some cases the authenticity will be a little impaired but the results are good.

Fenugreek
A spice used both in seed and ground form in Indian dishes, especially fish dishes. Obtainable from better supermarkets or oriental stores – but if you cannot obtain it omit from the recipe.

Garam masala
Literally 'dried spice mixture' in India, although a commercial preparation is now sold (see recipe). Garam masala is usually added to dishes towards the end of cooking – otherwise it can become slightly bitter.

Ghee
A type of clarified butter widely used in India as a cooking agent (see recipe). Butter or vegetable oil can be substituted.

Ginger
The root of the ginger plant is probably the single most important flavouring used in all oriental cooking – it is found in China, India, Japan and most of South-East Asia. Most recipes in this book call for fresh (green) ginger. To peel, scrape off the skin and any woody pieces and chop or grate the moist flesh. To store fresh ginger, wrap tightly, unpeeled, in plastic film or cover with dry sherry and leave in the refrigerator; it will keep for about six weeks. Although the taste is not really the same, *in extremis* ground ginger can be substituted for fresh – use about ½ teaspoon to 4cm./1½in. piece of fresh (green) ginger root. Obtainable from oriental stores and some specialty fruit and vegetable shops.

Lime	Sometimes used to provide a slightly sour flavour in Indian savoury dishes. If unobtainable lemon may be substituted.
Poppy seeds	Small seeds, both black and white, often used to thicken sauces slightly in Indian cooking. When added to a dish, they should first be cooked until they spatter slightly before adding other ingredients to the pan. Obtainable from oriental stores and better supermarkets.
Saffron	The world's most expensive spice and as a consequence perhaps used lovingly by almost every cuisine in the world. Made from the dried stamens of the crocus flower. It can be obtained in both strand and ground form – the strands should be soaked in warm water before using (see specific recipes for instructions). As a substitute for colour, turmeric can be used, but the flavour is very different.
Tamarind	The dried fruit of the tamarind tree, sold commercially in blocks. Used extensively in southern Indian cooking. Since the plant is somewhat fibrous, it is always soaked first, then strained and the tamarind water used rather than the fibrous pulp. See specific recipes for instructions on how to use.
Yogurt	One of the most popular cooking stocks in all of India. Commercial yogurt is perfectly acceptable but home-made is cheaper – and tastes better (see recipe). Always use plain yogurt as specified in the recipes.

RECIPE INDEX

INDIA